Style Me Vintage

accessories

Photography by Brent Darby

Naomi Thompson & Liz Tregenza

Style Me Vintage®

A guide to collectable hats, gloves, bags, shoes, costume jewellery & more

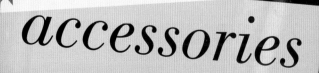

accessories

Contents

INTRODUCTION

Are you looking for small touches that will add a big impact to your outfit?

Are you looking to start a manageable vintage collection of accessible objects that you can enjoy now and potentially profit upon later?

Have you ever you ever lusted after a piece by a high-end couturier? Dior or Balenciaga, perhaps?

These are just some of the numerous benefits to collecting vintage accessories. We also believe herein lies the future of vintage collecting. As vintage aficionados we have both seen a gradual shift in the vintage retail and collecting landscape. On one hand clothes are becoming harder to find, and when you do they are rarely the affordable option they once were. It was inevitable that this was going to happen at some point. Demand has outstripped supply and the modern trend for wearing vintage styles means the pool has got smaller. This brings to the forefront the humble accessory, now at an exciting stage for new and old collectors alike. Thanks to the recent recognition that the vintage clothing market has received, these senescent handbags, scarves and even costume jewels are now desirable commodities in their own right. The market is ripe for both buyers and sellers.

Style-wise, accessories are the cherry on the cake for those who seek a period-accurate look, whilst also offering a source of complete style individuality for those who want to decorate themselves with something unique and special.

Accessories often transcend eras. The acquisition of 'classic' status means an item originally created over 80 years ago can look effortlessly chic paired with garments from any decade. And if that is not enough, accessories offer an affordable and thus easy way to buy into highly desirable vintage and heritage brands that would otherwise be out of reach.

'Money doesn't buy elegance. You can take an inexpensive sheath, add a pretty scarf, gray shoes, and a wonderful bag, and it will always be elegant.' Carolina Herrera

Accessories are easy to store, and are less prone to the perils of moth and rot. Depreciation due to wear is slower, so you can enjoy most purchases without the fear of excessive damage.

Many accessories can also act as beautiful decorative items for the home. Unlike clothes, that tend to require careful storing away in a wardrobe, many types of vintage accessory can be used to create fabulous displays. Think decorative piles of hatboxes or parasols, a mannequin covered with sparkling vintage brooches, or a vintage silk shawl draped over a bed.

But why do *we* love vintage accessories so much? The primary reason is because accessories are, quite simply, *accessible*. It doesn't matter what shape, size or age you are, anyone can appreciate, enjoy and collect vintage accessories. Vintage accessorizing is not necessarily about recreating the look of a certain era – we want to demonstrate how endlessly wearable vintage accessories can be, and how to become a savvy and knowledgeable collector. Quality over quantity, whilst not breaking the bank, is our mantra.

Opposite: These platform shoes by Lotus are one of Liz's most prized possessions. The original owner wore them to her wedding in 1948.

Below: Naomi: Growing up, I was in awe of my mother's oversized gold earrings. These Christian Lacroix earrings were purchased in Barcelona in the early 90s.

This book is organised by individual categories of accessory rather than by decade, so each chapter will maximise the knowledge imparted to you, the reader. We have combined accurate historical knowledge with styling, collecting and shopping tips and a smattering of 'insider views' and anecdotes from expert friends. Furthermore, if you are thinking 'I love the look of vintage accessories but I prefer to buy new', we have included a comprehensive list of vendors, stockists and indie designers of vintage-inspired accessories and future collectables.

So, the treasure hunt is back on! Car boots, eBay job-lots and charity shops are still teeming with items that are not as obvious as the now ubiquitous tea dress. Use this book to brush up on your brand names, learn how to distinguish your Bakelite from your Fakelite, or simply use it to inspire you to enter a new world of collecting.

Happy vintage hunting!

Naomi

Liz
x

Above: *The Red Hat*, fashion illustration by Gordon Conway, 1929. Note the matching cigarette holder and demi-parure of ring and cuff, designed to complement the red cloche hat.

Opposite: Liz: This cream 1930s embroidered bag, purchased by my mum in a charity shop when I was seven, started my obsession with vintage. The black example features a near identical design, but came from ebay in 2013.

Hats and Headpieces

'Cock your hat, angles are attitude' Sinatra

Women have been expected to cover their heads since the dawn of time, but it wasn't until the eighteenth century that the milliners of Milan took hat making out of the home and into the fashion arena for women.

There is no doubt that hats are now making a comeback. Once the preserve of churchgoers and royals, a new generation of talented milliners have reclaimed the art of hat wearing. These efforts were almost hampered by the worst thing to happen to the world of millinery: the rise and rise of the fascinator. The best thing to happen: the subsequent demise of the fascinator. The fascinator backlash culminated in the 2012 ban of said frothy headpieces at Royal Ascot, where they were deemed too informal. A headpiece with a base of four inches or more is now de rigueur.

Style-wise, donning a hat is the easiest way to make a strong and instant impact. It can change the way you hold yourself, how you walk and dramatically alter your silhouette. There are an abundance of plain felt and straw hats from the 1970s onwards to be found in thrift and charity shops, usually for very little. These make the ideal base for customising a hat to your tastes or altering a newer hat into an older style.

Types of Headwear

- Cloche
- Toque
- Tilt
- Tifter
- Juliet cap
- Pillbox
- Pancake
- Cartwheel
- Beret
- Turban
- Beehive
- Snood
- Veil
- Hair flower
- Decorative combs

HISTORY

Throughout the twentieth century, hat fashions were heavily influenced by the hairstyles of each era. The rebellious 1920s saw an outright rejection of the large, effervescent Edwardian creations in favour of close-fitting cloches and sparkling skull/Juliet caps that fitted perfectly over gamine Eton or Page Boy hair crops. In the 1920s it was vital that one's hat matched one's outfit and a number of the most prominent couturiers established 'atelier millinery' shops, run by professional milliners. This was a trend that continued up to the late 1960s as designers placed great importance on their hats. The fashion designer Cristóbal Balenciaga chose to take on the role of milliner himself by designing his own hats, whilst one of Christian Dior's muses, Mitzah Bricard, designed many of his.

All was not as austere as it may have seemed in the war-torn 1940s. In the UK, clothes and cloth came under the Utility Scheme and were rationed. However there were, surprisingly, a huge variety of hats available. Vibrant concoctions, embellished with feathers, artificial flowers and net, were popular, as these trimmings, along with any fabric less than three inches in width, were not rationed.

Very small hats known as 'tilt', 'doll' or 'toy' dominated the fashion scene in the 1940s – largely a legacy from the 1930s when hats were an integral part of an outfit. Worn perched on the forehead, they elongated one's silhouette and nestled

Opposite: The cloche (from the French for 'bell') is a hat often associated with the 1920s. In fact, the style was popular from the early 1910s right through to the 1930s. Cloches tend to be made from felt or straw.

Right: This delicate little 1940s fruit headpiece with veil came from America.

neatly in an up-do. In France these fun hats were dubbed *'pièce de résistance'* – in defiance of the austerity of Nazi occupation. Wartime patriotism also led to the increased popularity of the beret, influenced by military wear. As women were drafted in to help with the war effort, for practical purposes many took to wearing headscarves or snoods to cover unwashed hair or keep it under control when working.

The post-war period saw a relaxation of social conformity; this led to the demise of the daywear hat, but in turn bolstered the creative hat market. Popular styles included the 'pancake', which, as its name suggests, resembled a large flat pancake.

The new beehive hairstyle of the 1960s demanded hats that could perch neatly upon the heavily back-combed style. Particularly popular were veils or pillboxes (worn to the front of the head) and, confusingly, a hat named 'the beehive', which sat at the back of the head.

From the 1960s onwards, hats were generally only worn for special occasions, such as weddings or race meetings, or simply to protect against the weather. In the 1970s, floppy hats made from felt were a popular exception to the rule and were worn more generally.

Right: Simone wears a 1950s fine grey chapel hat of woven straw, covered with tiny white fabric flowers.

Opposite top: Sharon wears a 1940s silk scarf in her hair, fashioned into a bow.

Opposite below: Simone wears a 1950s black velvet pancake hat.

BRAND SPOTLIGHT

KANGOL

Kangol is a British brand famed for their berets. The company was formed in 1938 by Polish refugee Jacques Spreiregen. The name Kangol comes from the combination of three fabrics and techniques used by the brand - the 'K' from knitting, the 'ang' from angora, the 'ol' from wool (their name is nothing to do with their famous kangaroo logo!) During WWII their berets were hugely fashionable for men and women, and in the 1960s top designers such as Mary Quant and Pierre Cardin collaborated with the brand.

Right: A magazine advert for a Kangol design by Mary Quant in the 1960s.

Opposite top: A veiled creation designed by Lilly Daché, 1937.

Opposite bottom: A Jack McConnell design from 1976.

LILLY DACHÉ

Lilly Daché was a French milliner who found fame with her dramatic hats in the USA in the 1920s. She remained at the helm of her business until 1968, when her daughter, Suzanne, took over. Lilly produced hats for private clients and Hollywood studios alike, working with the famous costume designer Travis Banton and even designing Carmen Miranda's notorious turbans. Daché became well known for her draped turbans, but was also famed for her flower-shaped headpieces and coloured snoods. Later in her career she began designing clothing and other accessories, such as muffs and gloves, to go with her hats. Look out for Daché's two ready-to-wear hat lines 'Mme Lilly' and 'Dachéttes'.

TOP COLLECTORS' TIP

Jack McConnell Hats are highly sought-after pieces. The most valuable examples (often fetching over £250) have an actual red feather behind the label and were made by McConnell himself. McConnell's speciality was extravagant feather-covered hats, which he designed from the 1940s through to the 1980s.

Left: Naomi wears a 1960s orange feather-covered occasion hat, typical of the new shape of the 60s.

Opposite: Look for original labels and tags in headwear. The top label here is the original paper shop tag in a 1920s straw hat. Below it is an early 1960s Miss Dior 'Licence Chapeaux' label from a sequinned cap. Dior's lucrative licencing programme began in 1950. This saw his name placed on pretty much every accessory type included in this book. Whilst Miss Dior/Licence Dior items are highly sought-after, they are not as valuable as Dior originals.

Labels to look out for

- Jack McConnell
- Schiaparelli
- Dior
- Balenciaga
- Lilly Daché
- Caroline Reboux
- Aage Thaarup
- Edward Mann
- Mr John
- Stephen Jones
- Kangol
- Jacoll
- Bermona
- Piers Atkinson
- Otto Lucas
- Philip Treacy

TURBANS

Turbans are one of the fashion mainstays of the twentieth century; historically associated with India they were first adopted as an English fashion in the late 1700s and re-appeared in the Asian and Oriental influenced fashions of both the 1920s and 30s. During WWII turbans were worn on both sides of the Atlantic, often shaped in a 'V for Victory', framing the face. In the late 1950s, the turban, worn with a swing coat or dress, was the pinnacle of the fashionable triangular silhouette. London-based brand Biba resurrected the production of turbans in the 1970s, creating them in rainbow shades of shiny, stretchy Lurex. Turbans have stealthily crept back into modern wardrobes too (see our shopping page on p.154).

Styling tip: A plain stretch turban looks especially dramatic with the simple addition of a statement brooch in the middle.

Right: Susannah wears a plush green velvet 'Gloria' turban by contemporary Australian designer Alice Edgeley.

Opposite: 1929 Ilustration by Elsie Harding, featuring an elegant young woman with red hair just visible, tying a bandeau-style turban in gold colours around her head.

QUICK ERA GUIDE

20s – *Day:* Bell shaped, covering the ears and generally brimless except for summer versions. *Evening:* close fitting ornate caps

30s – Sculptural miniatures or brimmed flat straw

40s – Generally homemade or customised in the UK. Extravagant creations in France and the USA

50s – Small and close to the head

60s – Experimental and worn as a fashion accessory rather than a necessity for younger generations

70s – Not many popular styles. Predominantly wide brimmed and floppy, or turban-like

80s – Return of the veiled cocktail hat. Rigid, wide-brimmed millinery, as favoured by Lady Diana

Top: Mid-1950s blue velvet statement hat by Jeanne Pierre London.

Bottom: Late-1930s velvet cap-style hat with net bow. A Marten Model, made in England

Opposite: Late-50s–early-60s faux zebra fur pillbox hat with pompom.

DID YOU KNOW?

Hair flowers are a fashion trend often associated with the 1950s, but adding ornaments to the hair (fruit or flowers, for example) had been popular since the 30s, and hair combs made from sparkling paste or celluloid were de rigueur in the 20s.
In fact, hair flowers are particularly authentic to a 40s, rather than a 50s, look.

Left: A headdress made from original 1940s ribbons and felt flowers by Abbie Walsh.

Opposite: Jazz singer Billie Holiday, who made hair flowers a signature part of her look throughout the 1930s and 40s.

EXPERT: GEORGINA ABBOTT, OWNER OF ATELIER MILINERY, LONDON

For a vintage-look hat, it's fun to do it yourself. Atelier Millinery in London offer hat decorating and making courses. You can sift through drawers of original vintage milliner's accoutrements, from feather-weight veils to bird's wings.

1) Customise We regularly transform old ties into hatbands. I did one for my dad using a HUGE kipper tie of his, featuring 1920s-style ladies with cigarette holders and fox furs – not very PC, but VERY stylish. It now has a new lease of life on his panama.

Our favourite hat adornments ever are the vintage cherries stocked in our boutique. I say you can't have enough fruit on a vintage hat. Give me half a pound of cherries and some vintage veiling for good measure and I'll show you a great look.

2) It is possible to revitalise vintage pieces
One lady brought us her Grandmother's hat, which was completely squashed and not very appealing, until we cleaned and re-blocked it. It turned out to be just like the one you often see in photos of Coco Chanel. I didn't want to give it back.

We make a lot of bridal headpieces and often use old brooches, usually from a family member of the bride. It is a fabulous solution to the 'something old' question and gives new life to old pieces of costume jewellery that often languish in boxes never to be seen again. Even people who are not daily wearers of vintage enjoy the sentimental aspect of this upcycling.
www.ateliermillinery.com

STYLING TIPS

A felt hat of any era is the perfect blank canvas to work with. Our favourite is a wide-brimmed 1970s felt hat. They are still pretty easy to source from charity or thrift shops and can be made to look older. Dress it up with:
- Tied scarves
- Brooches and feathers
- The tie belt from a dress or jumpsuit, to match your hat to your outfit
- Hatpins
- Plastic fruit and flowers

Gloves

'It is presumably their relationship with the hand that gave gloves this symbolic value. Clenched in anger, pledged in loyalty, extended in friendship, plighted in love and even tied when powerless to act, the hand is busy in the most public, most private, of moments.'

Susan Vincent

The modern day glove is generally a woolly specimen dug out only in the depths of winter. Or, if one is feeling flush, it might be made of leather. Disregarding issues of warmth and practicality, gloves offer an instant touch of vintage authenticity or class to an outfit. The right gloves can make an outfit instantly recognisable as 'vintage'. Fun, and generally low cost, gloves can be picked up very easily secondhand. They are also one of the most common job lots in online auctions. From a styling point of view, matching your gloves to your tights, scarf, or hat can be a very neat way to pull an outfit together.

Types of Glove
- Matinee
- Opera
- Elbow
- Gauntlet
- Sleeve
- Day
- Driving

HISTORY

As early as 1929, the cultural historian Max von Boehn lamented that 'ladies hardly wear gloves at all'. Irrespective of this observation, gloves from the 1920s onwards were undoubtedly a fashion accessory. This is partly due to their transformation from an object of social necessity to a fashion choice. In the 1920s the variety of gloves on offer was striking; contrary to popular belief they were not restricted to neutral shades but in fact came in a wide variety of bright colours, fabrics and unusual shapes. One of the boldest was the gauntlet leather glove, which had an almost medieval look to it.

Gloves tend to come in three lengths; wrist 'matinee', elbow, and full length 'opera'. Up until the early 1960s the style of gloves worn was dictated by the time of day. Wrist-length gloves were suited to day dresses, worn in shades of cream and beige. Below-the-elbow gloves were designed to be worn with a short-sleeve evening dress. Above-the-elbow suited a more formal cocktail dress. Full-length were reserved for the most glamorous of events, in kid leather and satin, and worn with a strapless ball gown. Gloves retained their popularity partly through their ability to hide a multitude of sins, including large and aged hands. Vivien Leigh, for instance, disliked her hands, and hence wore gloves as often as possible.

Above: Jersey outfits by Bery in soft pastel shades, with hats and gloves to match, 1950.

Opposite: 1920s Art Deco gauntlet gloves of white kid leather.

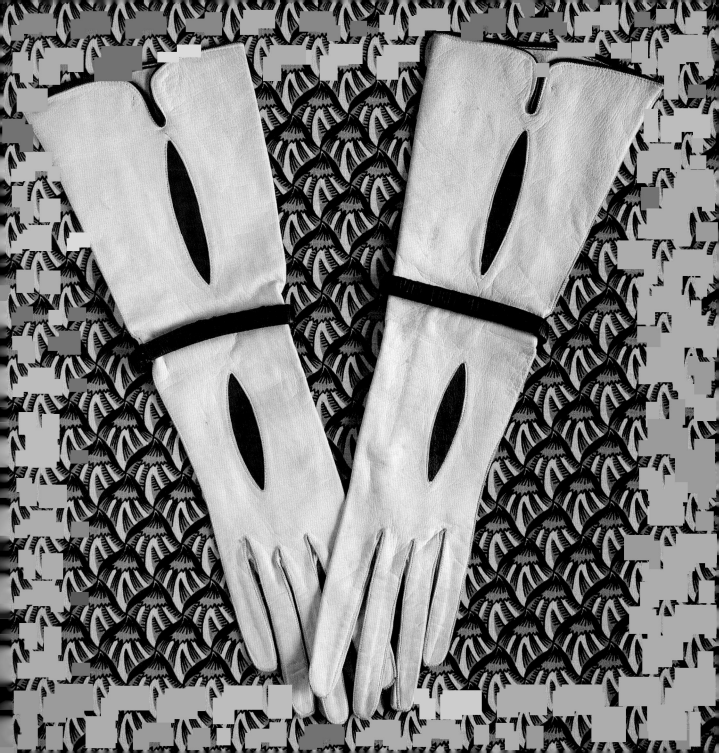

Dior's debut Corolle line of 1947 saw a return to Edwardian-inspired elegance, where ladies were expected to be ladies and gloves were once more essential. Day gloves were made in a variety of fabrics including cotton, net and lace. For younger girls such gloves were often frothy confections trimmed with ribbons and bows.

Another evening glove style was the 'sleeve', this fingerless, long glove had a triangular flap covering the hand and secured around the middle finger with elastic. These gloves were less restrictive than traditional opera gloves.

Gloves were rarely worn during the late 1960s and 1970s, other than by older women, but during the 1980s gloves had something of a renaissance. The popstar Madonna became a glove-wearing icon. In the video for her song 'Material Girl' she wore opera gloves that clearly took inspiration from the look of Marilyn Monroe in the 1953 film *Gentlemen Prefer Blondes*. She is also credited with catapulting fingerless lace gloves into fashion after her infamous MTV Music Award performance of 'Like A Virgin' in 1984.

Labels to look out for

- Dents (Dents' designed the gloves Queen Elizabeth II wore for her coronation)
- Shalimar
- Van Raalte
- Cornelia James
- Neyret
- Kayser

Opposite: An Edwardian glove box complete with its original accoutrements: buttonhook and ivory stretcher.

Right: Pink leather driving gloves from the 1960s perched on a turquoise vanity case of the same era.

HOW TO CLEAN LACE OR FABRIC GLOVES BY NAOMI

No matter how hard you try, gloves never stay clean. Apart from everyday dirt, mine always seem to get covered in lipstick (don't ask me why I pull them off with my teeth – this was once considered a great sign of disrespect). Soak in bicarbonate of soda and cold water first, then place in a pillowcase before machine-washing at 40 degrees. Make sure not to mix colours. For grease stains, add a dab of washing detergent before machine washing.

HOW TO CLEAN KID GLOVES BY LIZ

Cleaning kid leather gloves can be a nightmare, particularly the most popular cream and white ones, but here are a few top tips. Contrary to most advice found online, never use Vaseline, toothpaste or baby wipes to clean white kid leather. These can all cause damage, whether by yellowing the leather or causing it to dry out. Glycerin soap (solid translucent soap) is the best option for cleaning kid leather. Simply lather the soap in a bowl and use *only* the soapsuds to clean the gloves, don't put the gloves in the bowl itself! Lay flat to dry and away from direct heat. To get them looking tip-top again, once they are dry, massage a little beeswax-based conditioner into the gloves. Leave this to sit on the gloves for a day or two before lightly buffing with a soft brush.

Above: A selection of leather gloves in autumnal shades and from various designers including Dents, Leathercraft, Morley and Kenneth Rouse, 1950.

Opposite: An immaculate example of crochet gloves which were popular from the turn of the century to the 1930s. These have been finished with an intricate floral cuff.

GLOVE ETIQUETTE

Until the late 1960s, the wearing of evening gloves was dictated by strict etiquette. Here are just some of the rules.

1. Opera gloves should not be put on in public, only in the privacy of the home.
2. The shorter the sleeve of your dress, the longer your gloves should be.
3. Your gloves should be kept on when shaking hands or when dancing.
4. Gloves should only be worn when drinking if it is not easy to remove them in a polite manner.
5. Gloves should not be worn when eating, but once the meal is finished one should put them back on again.
6. Rings should not be worn over the top of gloves but bracelets can be.

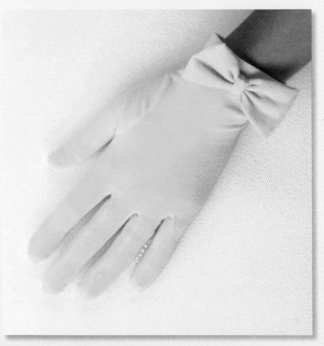

EXPERT: GENEVIEVE JAMES, CREATIVE DIRECTOR AND DAUGHTER OF FOUNDER, CORNELIA JAMES, ROYAL GLOVE MAKERS

Gloves are all about looking a million dollars without having to spend a million dollars. Good gloves can add leverage to your wardrobe, giving maximum return for minimum outlay. They shouldn't be the main story of an outfit, but gloves are often fundamental to the success of the main story.

You can wear them at any time of year. English summers offer a host of opportunities to dress up. Wearing gloves in the summer time can sound a little counterintuitive but, rather like drinking tea, a pair of cotton gloves can keep you feeling cool, calm and collected when it's baking hot.

If you're going the whole 'big hat route', gloves complete the picture. Why on earth would you not wear gloves? If you're more of a small hat/fascinator person, gloves offer an easy way to turn the 'dressed up' quotient up just a notch or two.

Gloves with a simple dress and dark glasses are great for achieving the Jackie O look and look effortlessly stylish.

The granting of the Royal Warrant in 1979 was Cornelia James's career highlight. The Royal Warrant is recognised the world over as a mark of quality and excellence and cannot be bought at any price.

www.corneliajames.com

Opposite: Selection of modern Cornelia James gloves.

Above A glove Cornelia James used to make in pure cotton. It was hand stitched and took a day to make, a real labour of love! Sadly, we stopped making hand-sewn cotton gloves about 10 years ago; we could no longer find the hand-sewers to make them (it is a dying craft).

INSIDER TOP TIP

A glove should be removed from the hand with care. Each finger should be gently tugged to avoid pulling the glove out of shape.

QUICK ERA GUIDE

20s – Crochet for day, though none at all for an *authentic* flapper look

30s – Gauntlet Gloves (though these have been around since the time of Elizabeth I)

40s – Often unworn due to relaxed dress codes

50s – Wrist or 'bracelet' gloves

60s – Small and neat, by now the preserve of church-going ladies

70s – Virtually unworn

80s – Big revival supplemented by the trend for fingerless gloves

The only type of fashion glove that has remained in continuous favour since the Regency era is the opera glove.

Opposite: Model in green cotton lace dress with 'late-day' neckline and white elbow-length gloves, 1954.

Above: Accessories from 1967. Model wears orange earrings by KJL, beige kid gloves with orange flower by Kislav, scarf by Sant' Angelo for Sally Gee, orange canvas bag by Tano and pouch by Lesco Lona.

Shoes

*'Give a girl the correct footwear and
she can conquer the world.'*

Bette Midler

Good footwear will last and protect your posture. It's no coincidence that quality-made shoes from the 30s, 40s and 50s can still be found in box-fresh condition, whereas the cheaper versions from the 60s onwards have long since perished. However, in the current shoe market there has been a return to old-school methods and standards of quality. In the past twenty years many cheap shoe brands have gone out of business, paving the way for a resurgence of the high-end, artisanal shoe. Names such as Terry de Havilland, Charlotte Olympia, Sophia Webster and Beatrix Ong immediately spring to mind. You only need to look at the popularity of the Louboutin to understand the kind of sums that women (and men) are willing to part with in the name of superior footwear.

Types of Shoe
- Wedge
- Louis heel
- Platform
- Stiletto
- Kitten heel
- Espadrille
- Court shoe or Pump
- Clog
- Pilgrim
- Mary Jane
- T-Bar
- Slipper
- Mule
- Sandal
- Ballet flat
- Saddle
- Brogue
- Cowboy boot

HISTORY

As hemlines rose during the 1920s, shoes were on display more than ever before. This led to an influx of shoe designs in a huge variety of colours and styles. For evening there was a prevalence of gold and silver kid leather, often accented with paste-encrusted heels to match the sparkling dresses. Footwear design was influenced by the big dance crazes of the era such as the Charleston and Bunny Hop. The vigorous dance moves (considered rather risqué for the time) demanded shoes with bars and straps to help them stay on the feet. A completely new arrival was the T-bar, born in 1922.

For daywear the androgynous sports oxford and two-tone spectator shoes (both a type of brogue) were hugely popular. The Mary Jane shoe was also a key fashion trend. These childlike shoes with a bar across the instep perfectly matched the juvenile image that the flapper girls wished to evoke.

Into the 30s, styles remained relatively similar but with more of the foot on show: peeptoes and slingbacks became key shoe features. The platform began its assault on fashion in the mid 1930s, taking its roots from wedged sandals worn for the beach. Italian shoe designer Salvatore Ferragamo is credited with turning the platform into a high fashion accessory. He created his shoes from unconventional materials such as cork, raffia and wood. Ferragamo estimated in 1939 that 86 per cent of women's shoes had a wedge or platform heel. Platforms remained popular during the 1940s perfectly complementing the square shouldered military look that dominated fashion. In America shoes made from fabric rather than leather or rubber were not restricted under L-85 (the US ration system). This led to the elevation of the traditional Spanish espadrille, famously worn by Lauren Bacall in the 1948 film *Key Largo*.

After WWII there was an explosion of shoe styles, with many women opting to wear dainty, elegant and, eventually, more erotic styles. As the 1950s progressed, a woman's heel

Page 45: Daniel Green have producing slippers since 1882. An advert for this style, "Frou Frou" from 1939, states that they were produced in "blossom pink and poppy red" amongst other colours. They cost the princely sum of $8.50. Not cheap for a pair of shoes meant to be worn in the bedroom.

Opposite: Liz (left) wears a pair of 1920s lace-up brogues, traditionally worn for sport. This style is known as a Ghillie brogue. Naomi (right) wears a pair of 1940s Lotus tassled oxblood brogues.

Right: A pair of 1940s satin mules by collectable label Delman.

became more and more slender until it reached its slimmest, the stiletto – most commonly associated with the French designer Roger Vivier. The reason why heels became so slim was all a matter of technology. The breakthrough came in Italy where heels were created using a metal core inserted into the shaft of a plastic heel shell, enabling style and, crucially, stability.

In contrast to the sky-high heels of the 1950s, there was also a trend towards flat shoes, particularly those worn by beatniks, who helped to popularise both the ballet pump and the saddle shoe. Flats with capris, peddle pushers or cigarette pants make for a very chic Audrey Hepburn look.

Footwear in the 60s was, on the whole, low. One of the most prevalent styles was the square-toed pilgrim. The 1960s saw the return of the boot, which had been in the fashion doldrums since the 1920s. No longer were boots for purely practical purposes. Mary Quant's short boots were especially innovative, made from transparent plastic with an interior layer of cotton jersey. Shoes of the 1960s also paid homage to those of the 1920s with the return of a flat Mary Jane.

TOP TIP

Not sure if your shoes are genuine 1950s? Shoes of this era almost always have metal tips on the heels.

Opposite: A selection of 1960s low-heeled pilgrim shoes by Miss Holmes and Rayne.

Above: A Russell and Bromley magazine advert from the 1940s.

In the 1970s a more exaggerated platform reigned supreme, this time adopted by two fashion tribes wearing the style in very different ways. Hippies wore stacked heel platforms and clogs made in raffia and wood. In London, companies such as Biba, Terry de Havilland and Chelsea Cobbler began producing ultra-high glam platforms in shiny metallic leathers and even, in Biba's case, encrusted in diamanté. In America, Candie's made mule-type clog shoes that were particularly fashionable amongst teens.

The 1980s was the decade of the power shoe, which was both extremely high and pointy. For those who preferred a more comfortable shoe there was also the new cone-shaped lower heel often attached to a sensible pump. In complete contrast, anti-fashion shoes such as Dr. Martens (army-style boots with air cushioned soles available since 1960) and Converse sneakers (first developed in 1917) became popular. These styles had been worn by women since the late 1970s, increasing in popularity in the 1980s, although they still remained a sub-cultural rather than mainstream style.

Above: A classic example of 1970s platform boots.

Opposite: 1980s court shoes, channelling the style of the Dutch painter Mondrian, by St. Michael (former brand of Marks & Spencer).

TOP TIP

Satin shoes may look great for a display but left in sunlight can discolour in a matter of days. Liz learnt this the hard way with a beautiful pair of turquoise satin Rayne shoes.

FOOTWEAR RATIONING

When searching for British 1940s shoes, pairs with the CC41 logo often turn up. CC41 is generally recognised as standing for Controlled Commodity 1941. Garments and accessories produced under this scheme were official utility items and conformed to a set of regulations that ensured goods were both well made and hard-wearing. Regulations of 1942 stipulated that such shoes could not have peep toes or heels higher than two inches. CC41 shoes are generally practical, unless they are post-war examples when regulations were relaxed.

Footwear was also rationed in the US although they are not marked in a visible manner like their UK counterparts. In February 1943, the US introduced rationing of leather shoes. Each man, woman and child could purchase up to three pairs of leather shoes a year, though by 1944 this had been reduced to only two. During this time only six shades of leather were produced: black, white, navy blue and three shades of brown. Unsurprisingly these were not as desired as their cheerful cork, raffia and fabric counterparts.

TOP TIP

Look out for shoes with leather lining. These are often of the best quality.

Opposite: Utility footwear was made from incredibly sturdy leather, shoes tended to be leather-lined, double-soled and double-stitched. These features ensured that a pair of CC41 shoes would last a number of years despite regular wear.

Labels to look out for

- Dolcis
- Lilley and Skinner
- Bally
- Charles Jourdan
- Keds
- Bernie Mev
- Jones
- Ravel
- Russell and Bromley (Stuart Weitzman and Beverly Feldman)
- Chelsea Cobbler
- Lotus
- Roger Vivier
- Ferragamo
- Terry de Havilland
- Hush Puppies
- Camper
- Daniel Green
- Carmina
- John Lobb
- Rayne
- Delman
- Candie's
- Bata
- Perugia
- F. Pinet
- Saxone
- Shellys

Opposite: Mules, long associated with the boudoir, became popular evening shoes in the 1950s. As heel height increased, the single strapped mule became more difficult to keep on. This led to the invention of the iconic 'spring-o-lator' in 1954. This leather and elastic insert in the sole of the shoe pushed the foot upwards and kept it in contact with the strap of the mule. These are a modern example by Miss LFire.

Right: 1980s Beverley Feldman for Russell and Bromley plastic mules with floating cherries in their heels. Note the equally opulent (and typically 80s) box.

BRAND SPOTLIGHT
RAYNE AND DELMAN

Rayne were one of the leading British manufacturers of shoes, holding the Royal Warrant from 1936. The company's origins lie as theatrical costumiers, starting in 1885. However, by the 1920s Rayne were selling their exclusive shoes in their own shops.

Edward Rayne, grandson of the original founders, helped to catapult the brand to international fame. It was during his tenure that Rayne shoes were at their most elegant and expertly crafted, using American production techniques and soles to make the shoes more comfortable and flexible. The sizes and fittings were also based on American standards. Rayne had designers and makers in America, many of whom were first generation Italians instilled with the superior skills of Italian craftsmanship.

The brand is also well known for their collaborations with a number of leading designers of their time, including Norman Hartnell, Jean Muir and Bill Gibb.

Rayne is strongly linked to the eponymous US brand Delman. Established by Herman Delman in 1919, the brand was worn by the likes of Marilyn Monroe and Marlene Dietrich. Rayne held the UK licence for producing Delman shoes from 1935. In 1961 Rayne purchased the Delman brand and Edward Rayne became president of the Delman salons in America. This meant that Edward was one of only a small number of people at the time that personally directed a fashion business in both New York and London.

'Finding a vintage pair of Rayne's in their original iconic yellow box is one of the single greatest pleasures I have as a buyer of vintage accessories.' Liz

Opposite: These Rayne black satin shoes were purchased for just £4 in a charity shop.

Above: These 1950s court shoes by Lotus are one of their most popular styles: the "Caribbean court". Liz likes them so much that she owns five pairs in different colours and fabrics!

Opposite: Late 1930s black satin shoes, trimmed with gold kid leather and paste-encrusted buckles, by Delman.

QUICK ERA GUIDE

20s – Ballet-inspired slippers with a Louis heel

30s – Brogues, T-bar shapes, platforms

40s – Sturdy platforms in the UK, decorative non-leather shoes in the US

50s – Stilettos, pointy kitten heels

60s – Boots, pilgrim shoes, flat Mary Janes

70s – Clogs, platforms

80s – Power shoes or pumps

LETS TALK ABOUT PLASTIC

Particularly from the 1950s onwards, imitation leather was used to make both shoes and bags, this synthetic can become 'sticky' (or tacky) with age. Sadly this means that the plastic is slowly decomposing and is beyond repair. Avoid like the plague.

If plastic does dry out it tends to become brittle. This can be partly prevented by storing your shoes in natural cloth bags.

SHOE CLIPS

Removable clips, buckles, rosettes and other adornments have long been used to embellish shoes. This trend died down in the 1980s, but a number of modern makers and creators are resurrecting this idea.

A pair of simple court shoes can be transformed to match any outfit by adding clips. Try these ideas:

• Source a vintage pair of clips (see the picture on pages 62–63 of an example from the 1930s);

• Buy newly-made ones (the shoe company Van Dal still produce them) or many Etsy sellers now supply them online.

• Make your own. This can be achieved by purchasing the studded clips and adding any decoration you wish, from pom poms to fans. Glue or sew them on firmly.

• Recycle old brooches or lightweight clip-on earrings with a sturdy clasp.

Opposite: A 1950s fruit-covered novelty box bag and modern Miss L Fire wedges, adorned with strawberries, which have more than a flavour of 40s and 50s shoes.

Above: A selection of shoe clips and vintage earrings, all of which can be used to transform plain court shoes.

Left: Plain black suede 1950s court shoes accessorised with rare "apple juice" Bakelite bow-shaped shoe clips from the 1930s.

BRAND SPOTLIGHT
TERRY DE HAVILLAND

A focus on style versus fashion has been the key to the ever evolving success and reinvention of Terry de Havilland, both for the man himself and his eponymous brand. By the age of five Terry was hammering wooden dowels into the three-tier wedges his father was making to sell on the black market and to the Windmill Girls of the 1940s. After a stint in Rome as an actor, during which Terence John Higgins became Terry de Havilland, he was called back to the family business in 1960, swapping *la dolce vita* to help meet the huge demand for his father's winklepickers – stiletto-heeled versions for the girls and Cuban heels for the boys.

In the late 60s Terry rediscovered some of the components used by his father during the war and together they restarted the three-tier wedge process, this time with Terry's flamboyant designs. These spectacularly matched the mood and the fashions of the era.

By the 1970s Terry had taken over the business after his father was tragically killed in an industrial accident. Rather than languish in grief, Terry and his mother Kitty worked through their heartache to ensure the family business soared. Thanks to his then father-in-law the brand made its way across the pond to New York and by 1972 the opening of his legendary Kings Road shop had cemented his presence firmly in the rock-and-roll folklore of the era.

The opening party was "a riot of champagne, cocaine and caviar packed out with all the faces, from rock stars and groupies to fashion journalists and gangsters."

It is well known that de Havilland provided footwear for many of the key players of the era, earning him the 'rock-and-roll cobbler' crown, but some of his less publicised encounters are the ones that stick in Terry's mind: "I made Rudolph Nureyev (the famed ballet dancer) knee-high platform python boots. The next customer who came in asking for them was Demis Roussos (the larger-than-life Greek operatic prog rocker). He had seen Nureyev wearing them and wanted the same ones. You couldn't imagine designing such boots for two such different people."

From the 1970s onwards, Terry designed and sold shoes under various monikers. In 1980 he set up a new label called

> *'Terry de Havilland shoes
> are undoubtedly magical.
> They have experience.
> This generation pinch their
> mothers' — and they always
> have a story attached.'*
>
> Liz de Havilland

Kamikazi, which made shoes for punks and goths. Think heavily buckled winklepickers adorned with skulls, studs and spikes.

By the 1990s, Terry and his future wife Liz were working under the Magic Shoes brand. After a chance meeting with the photographer Bob Carlos Clarke, he introduced the first commercially produced line of latex boots for the fetish market, manufacturing them for both men and women.

After a 20 year hiatus, Terry noted: "I had more presence in museums than retail shops and this needed to be redressed." The De Havilland brand was promptly resurrected for the 21st century. Today the De Havillands are based in a studio in East London where they continue to create ready-to-wear and couture collections for high profile clients and aficionados alike.

Opposite: Terry de Havilland plastic and snakeskin platform sandals with diamanté buckles from the 70s.

Above: The Margaux, such a classic at 41 years old, goes with everything. Look out especially for the high wedge python version.

TOP COLLECTOR'S TIP
Look out for the TDH range of Spring-o-lator ready-to-wear mules for 2015.

Costume Jewellery

'If I was a woman, I would be dressed in the same thing for a month and just change my hat and gloves. Maybe my shoes too; yes, I see what you mean, but really, it's jewels that change an outfit.'

Manolo Blahnik

Jewellery has always been desired and thus will always be collected. 'Costume' jewellery may seem like the poor relation of its 'fine' counterparts but is much easier to collect. The right pieces often command astronomical sums yet, if luck strikes, can still be found for relatively little. Furthermore, you don't need to be an expert in hallmarks and carats to build a collection of considerable value, although brushing up on makers' marks and early plastics will certainly stand you in good stead. Style-wise, costume jewellery can be the smallest addition to any outfit, vintage or otherwise, but can make the strongest impact.

Types of Jewellery

- Bangles
- Rings
- Bracelets
- Necklaces
- Brooches
- Cardigan clips
- Chokers
- Earrings
- Pendants
- Armlets

HISTORY

The 1920s witnessed a completely new direction for jewellery, with 'costume' items firmly establishing themselves as viable alternatives to real jewels for even the wealthiest women. Nancy Cunard, the shipping heiress, became a style icon with her avant-garde 'barbaric' jewellery. Bangles in particular, like those worn by Nancy, were a fashion symbol of the 1920s. Worn either stacked up the arm or just a single bangle higher up (an armlet), they were restrictive and quite cumbersome, as was much of the jewellery in the 1920s. This was in direct contrast to the new female silhouette, finally freed from the corset. African tribal items were the dominant trend. The snake motif was also significant (again a symbol of restriction), appearing in bangles, necklaces and brooches.

Above: Nancy Cunard (1896–1965), heiress to the Cunard Line fortune, enjoyed the friendship of avant-garde writers and artists, and is seen here in her trademark 'barbaric' bangles in the 20s.

Left: A typical 1920s snake armlet embossed with tiny paste stones.

Large chunky bangles were made from a variety of materials, although the most popular at the time (and today most collectible) were Bakelite. This formaldehyde-based resin was invented by Leo Bakeland in 1907 but was only widely used for jewellery from the 1920s onwards. From the 1930s, Catalin, a type of imitation Bakelite, was produced.

Initially known as the 'gaudy brother' of Bakelite, Catalin could be produced in brighter colours and was sold at cheaper prices by the popular American 'five and dime' stores.

Hollywood defined the modern glamorous look of the 1930s and had a major influence on jewellery design. Glittering paste complemented the outfits worn by the starlets of the day such as Joan Crawford and Jean Harlow. This look could be recreated by women everywhere. Paste jewellery was often multi-functional and could be worn in a variety of ways, as dress clips, brooches or pendants. There was also a Victorian style revival, with delicate pieces inset with marcasite or Czech glass in dainty filigree settings.

Top: A 1930s Art Deco black plastic buckle brooch.

Right: Front cover of The Delineator, March 1927, featuring an illustration of a fashionable young woman wearing a matching pink dress and cloche hat, set off with a parure of emerald jewellery.

Opposite: 1930s glass necklaces and early plastic decorative belt buckles of the same era.

March 1927   25c
Delineator

Sophie Kerr
Frances Parkinson Keyes · Eleanor Hallowell Abbott
Smart Spring Fashions

Patriotic pieces were favoured in the 1940s. Pins depicting flags of the Home Nations were worn in support of the war effort. Brooches were a particularly thrifty way for women to update tired outfits and were manufactured in abundance.

The 1940s also hailed a new dawn of American jewellery designers, the most prominent being Miriam Haskell. Haskell, and her designer Frank Hess, produced exclusive handcrafted creations. The pieces produced by the brand in the 1940s demonstrate their innovative use of materials such as plastic beads and shells. Beads were drawn together in elaborate three-dimensional creations such as fruits and flowers.

Many novelty pieces at this time were produced in Bakelite and celluloid – an early plastic, originally used as a substitute for ivory, which is now much-collected. Novelty plastics continued to be a strong trend right through the 1950s. The most popular themes (and now some of the most sought-after) included jewellery sets adorned with bright and colourful fruits and a veritable menagerie of animals.

Above: A 1950s plastic and glass novelty domino necklace.

Opposite: Sweetheart brooches, such as this American example, were worn by young girls all over the world in homage to their boyfriends or fiancés serving in the war.

The 1950s was a decade of sparkle, encouraged partially by the development in 1955 of the kaleidoscopic Aurora Borealis stones by Swarovski. Shimmering jewellery by Dior was amongst the most striking and throughout the decade Dior worked with some of the leading names in jewellery design, including Henkel & Grosse, Kramer and Mitchell Maer.

Cocktail rings were big news (literally!) in the 1950s and many women wore huge-scale rings on top of dramatic opera gloves, despite etiquette suggesting you should not.

TOP TIP

1950s jewellery etiquette: clip earrings (generally rounded, though ornate) for daytime; long and dangly earrings only suitable for evening.

Above: A 1950s–60s sterling silver and pearl cocktail ring, designed by Italian jeweller Benedetto Panetta, in its original olive-green velvet box. Panetta's background was in fine jewellery and many of his costume items reflected his training.

Opposite: A selection of cocktail rings, from left to right: 1970s amethyst coloured glass inlaid into a gold dragonfly setting (Naomi's own), late 1950s large blue glass rectangle surrounded with rhinestones (from Passionate About Vintage), 1930s clear blue oval stone (from Marjorie May Vintage).

The sparkling parures and demi-parures of the 1950s were still popular in the 1960s, although they became quite oversized and were mainly worn with dramatic full-length cocktail dresses. A 'parure' is a set of at least 3 matching items of jewellery, designed to be worn all at once.

The word *parure* comes from Old French, meaning 'to adorn', and was first used in the 17th century. It originated as a fine jewellery term but is now widely used by vintage costume jewellery collectors to describe jewellery sets. A 'demi-parure' is a two-piece set. It is also possible to find 'married parures', these are jewellery sets with two matching or similar pieces, that look good together, but were perhaps not originally made by the same person or at the same time. The most lavish parure is the 'full' or 'grand parure' – a whole set, designed to be worn together, consisting of at least four pieces of matching jewellery.

Numerous firms throughout the twentieth century have produced parures, but some of the best examples were made by firms such as Miriam Haskell, Schiaparelli and Trifari.

Above and opposite: The sets pictured here are 'demi-parures', intentional two-piece jewellery sets. Both these demi-parures consist of earrings and a bracelet, but a demi-parure may also consist of a necklace and brooch.

TOP TIP
Today Lucite sets of a 'clamper' bangle and matching earrings are very desirable on the collectors market.

Despite the lingering popularity of sparkling stones, 1960s jewellery was primarily made from plastics such as Perspex. 'Flower power' motifs (a term coined by Allen Ginsberg) were everywhere in the 1960s, applied to dresses, handbags or even underwear. Bold, brightly-coloured flower jewellery completed the look, enamel examples are particularly good. It is always worth looking out for the mid-90s pieces that recreated this look as they can still be picked up incredibly cheaply.

Our favourite look of the 1970s was the explosion of Navajo-inspired jewels, which is currently a huge trend. Think turquoise set in chunky silver, opaque stones in reddish hues, colourful micro-beads, feathers, leather and Aztec prints. Smaller trends included an art deco revival initiated by Kenneth Jay Lane, striking modernist pendants such as those produced by Italian designer Elsa Peretti and an abundance of butterflies, beads and craft items.

Above: A 1960s plastic cube and ball bracelet with matching monochrome earrings.

Opposite: A selection of 20th century Navajo-inspired jewellery. From right to left: a 1920s micro-beaded necklace, 1970s bracelet of a similar construction, and a modern set (consisting of sterling silver mosaic and bead earrings, necklace and ring).

TOP TIP

A small pair of pliers will become your friend! These are great for tightening up loose fittings.

CHANEL
BOUTIQUE

Punk began to have a major influence on jewellery towards the end of the 1970s and was watered down for the mainstream market with pieces made to look like padlocked ropes and chains. Following on from this darker look were a prevalence of crucifixes, popularised by Christian Lacroix. They were widely copied on the high street and by smaller designers. This trend continued well into the mid-90s.

The 1980s was a decade of ultimate fakery in terms of jewellery. High-end jewellery brands were using obviously faux gemstones and metals, harking back to Coco Chanel's love of fake in the 1920s. If it wasn't over-the-top, oversized and overstated, it didn't belong in the 80s.

Above: An early 1990s Chanel advert featuring their famed faux pearls.

Opposite: Marcasite and sterling silver 1930s bat brooch, mounted on a chain. Naomi's grandfather bought it at the local car boot sale for her grandmother Jean. A timeless example of gothic style.

COLLECTING SPOTLIGHT: CAMEOS

Cameos are miniature positive reliefs that are then made into items of jewellery. This is in contrast to an intaglio piece, which is carved into the back and viewed from the front. To put it simply, cameos are works of art, designed to be worn.

Cameos have existed at least as far back as Roman times, though they last reached a peak in popularity in the 1970s, after which they went out of fashion. Cameos are seen adorning all jewellery types, but the most commonly found these days are brooches. Traditionally they are carved from shell, but can also be made from glass or moulded in plastic, with the better versions inlaid into a metal frame decorated with a pearl or filigree detail. Common themes are Greek and Roman profiles or dainty ethereal characters. 1970s revival cameos are often made of moulded plastic featuring reliefs of ladies with pert noses and comedic cascading curls.

Style-wise, cameos have always looked attractive pinned at the base of the neck, as the centrepiece of a collar or high-necked blouse – a Victorian fashion that is still popular today.

Left: One of the most popular brands of the 1980s was Butler and Wilson, a firm still in operation today. It was set up by Nicky Butler and Simon Wilson, who began their career together as antique dealers in the 1960s. They are best known for producing overblown diamanté pieces, with a nod towards older design, such as these beautiful spider earrings.

Opposite: A Victorian corset-maker's bust makes an elegant display stand for a collection of mid-century paste brooches.

KNOW YOUR BAKELITE FROM YOUR FAKELITE

There are various tests to ascertain whether Bakelite is genuine or not. There is a lot of contradictory opinion on the topic, although personally we use the following methods.

THE RUB TEST

The heat generated from rubbing a Bakelite item should cause it to emit a formaldehyde-like chemical smell. This is a quick and easy method when shopping at thrift or charity shops, car-boots and yard sales. It is however bad form to start rubbing pre-identified items - always ask the vendor first.

A more reliable technique is to run the item under hot water for a minute to see if the smell appears. This carries a higher risk of damage than the Rub Test but if you are really unsure as to whether an item is genuine Bakelite or not it is worth a go.

SIMICHROME POLISH

Many blogs also recommend Simichrome polish, a non-abrasive cream mainly used for cleaning metals. It is good for shining plastics, but can be damaging too. The Bakelite test with Simichrome works in the following way: The pink-toned polish will turn yellow when applied to genuine Bakelite.

Please note: Unless you are testing a Bakelite piece it should not emit a smell at all. If a piece has a chemical vinegary smell then walk away! This means the plastic is degrading. Not only are these pieces likely to degrade further, they can often kick-start the process in other plastic items stored alongside them. This is why the degradation process is sometimes called 'the disease'.

TOP BAKELITE TIPS

1. There is no such thing as white Bakelite.
2. Bakelite rarely has seams or mould marks, this is a characteristic of hard plastic.
3. Gently knocking together two Bakelite bangles should produce a distinctive 'clunk' sound.
4. The carved pieces are the most sought-after.

PEARLS

A string of pearls is a staple of the vintage wardrobe and has never really gone out of favour. They come in various necklace styles: collar, princess, matinee, opera or rope. Popularity highlights include the 1920s; think long multiple strands. In contrast, the 1950s favoured a choker-style double or triple strand with a statement clasp. Keep a look out for the Majorica brand. Produced on the Island of Majorca since 1890, these are amongst the best imitation pearls you can buy.

Above: American actress Claudette Colbert in pearls, 1928.

Opposite: An unusual fairy-shaped brooch by French designer Lea Stein. Stein began producing her collectable Art Deco-inspired plastic pieces in the 1960s, the most famous of which is probably her fox design. Stein pieces are immediately recognisable for their V-shaped metal clasps inscribed with 'Lea Stein Paris'.

EXPERT TIPS: NATALIE LEON, OWNER OF PASSIONATE ABOUT VINTAGE AND VINTAGE JEWELLERY SPECIALIST

- Condition is key. Look carefully at the front and back of the piece. Is there any kind of visible damage? Has it been repaired? It's always better to buy something that hasn't been repaired and is in good condition.

- Buy the best you can afford.

- Trust your instincts. If you can already picture how you will wear it, the outfit it will complete, the dress it matches, then this is the piece for you.

- Most importantly, buy what you love!

www.passionateaboutvintage.co.uk

Handbags
and Purses

'No one should make fun of anyone else's handbag choices.'
Hilary Clinton

The handbag is the ultimate twentieth century accessory, whether vintage or otherwise. Nothing retains its worth and desirability like a good bag. Bags are a functional way to add a touch of vintage kudos to an everyday outfit. Looked after properly with gentle use and care, a good vintage bag will go the distance both in terms of use and investment. For example, 1970s Gucci can still be found for less than the price of average high street handbags, whilst Lucite box-bags increase in value year-on-year.

Styles of Handbag

- Clutch
- Doctor's/Gladstone
- Box
- Bucket
- Minaudière
- Satchel
- Tote
- Vanity case
- Carpet
- Dorothy
- Bowling
- Envelope
- Gasmask
- Matinée
- Tapestry/
  Petit point
- Shoulder
- Pochette
- Basket
- Reticule

HISTORY

The handbags that we predominantly see today came into their own during the 1920s. In the 1920s and 30s delicately embroidered clutch bags covered in glass seed beads and sequins (or *pailettes*) were popular. With just enough room to carry your make-up and a mirror, these bags were so small that today we might consider them purses. The best examples were often embroidered in France or Belgium, and have tiny labels saying so. Their patterns vary, but many contain motifs inspired by Art Nouveau (floral and swirls) or Art Deco (geometric patterns). These bags perfectly complemented both the beaded flapper dresses of the 1920s and the swishing bias cut gowns of the 1930s. But why were these bags so small? To draw attention to a ladies well manicured hands! These tiny bags were primarily a European fashion trend, until 1924 when American women, possibly tired of being satirised for their use of large bags, also adopted them.

Previous page and top: A good way to date a bag is to take close look at the lining. In pre-1940s bags, such as these examples, it is often more opulent than the exterior: vibrant silks in floral or novelty motifs, often edged with ric rac or tiny flowers.

Left: Liz: When I purchased this 1950s *petit point* bag it was filled with little notes. One informed me that the bag is French and is formed of over 96,000 stitches!

Opposite: A trio of 1920s and 1930s seed-beaded bags. The top example is Japanese, made for European market, whilst the others are both French.

Compact handbags were highly desirable from the 1920s to the 1960s. In the 1920s ladies often carried vanity dance purses, which were tiny bags in hard materials such as celluloid based on Japanese *inrø*. In the 1930s the name *minaudiére* was coined for these little bags that combined all the accoutrements of a handbag and a powder compact in one. The name *minaudiére* comes from the French '*minauder*' (to show-off, pose) and was patented by the jewellery firm Van Cleef and Arpels.

Animal skins were hugely popular for both day and evening bags in the 1930s, and were commonly fashioned from reptile skins, usually crocodile and lizard. This trend started as a response to the lack of leather available during the First World War. The 1930s was also a decade of understated elegance in hand bags, black leather was combined with chrome fittings in classic Art Deco shapes, and, most importantly, bags were built to last.

TOP TIP

Never store plastic (including Lucite and Bakelite) items in plastic. If you can, wrap in acid-free tissue paper, and store them somewhere dark, cool and dry.

Above: Elephant clutch bag, c.1925–35. Colourful bags such as this were produced in the Far East for the European market to satisfy a demand for items depicting overseas colonies and oriental motifs.

Opposite: A 1930s *minaudiére* handbag with compartments for powder, cigarettes and other small necessities.

Left: Highly ornate 1930s clutches. The red example is made from wool with ceramic tiles set into the clasp. The gold example is embroidered with Asian floral motifs and the clasp is set with faux jade stones.

Towards the end of the 1930s, leather was again in short supply. This saw the advent of a new fabric, cordé (contrary to popular assumption 'cordé' is the name of the fabric, rather than a brand name). Cordé (or sometimes Korday, which *is* a brand name) is made from rows of gimp-strands of silk or wool wound around a wire or cord core and stitched to a fabric base. These bags remained fashionable into the 1950s, and were often accented with Lucite pulls or handles. In the 1940s, magazine adverts described cordé as the 'dressiest, handsomest and most hardwearing of all handbag fabrics.'

Handbags in the 1940s were also known for their functionality. Bags themselves were not rationed, but were often prohibitively expensive. If buying new, satchel styles and military-influenced shapes were the most popular choice. Otherwise women resorted to homemade examples using scraps of fabric, felt or bags made from raffia.

By September 1939 – the outbreak of World War II – 38 million gasmasks had been distributed across the UK. In response some companies designed elegant cases for women who did not want to carry around the utilitarian cardboard box that they came in. These are now extremely rare.

Novelty was the buzzword of the 1950s, particularly with the emerging 'teenage' market. Bags were made from a wide variety of original materials in crazy shapes and colours. Straw bags were particularly popular in both France and Japan, whilst all around the world plastic was being woven to resemble straw.

TOP TIP

Vintage bags are often lined in suede, which is a notoriously difficult fabric to clean. Always keep make-up etc. in a separate, sealed bag within your vintage handbag, to avoid damaging the lining.

Box-bags were produced in a wealth of materials including wood, metal, Perspex, Plexiglas and most importantly Lucite – a plastic first developed in 1931 by DuPont for military use. In the 1950s, mainly in the United States, Lucite was one of the top materials for bags. The vast majority of the best Lucite bags were produced in New York and Florida by companies such as Llewellyn Inc., Dorset Rex and Wilardy – who were famed for their bags featuring lace, crushed seashells and glitter. Initially the bags were quite expensive; but as they became popular, cheaper versions became widely available.

Also fashionable at this time were *petit point* bags that were finely embroidered with miniscule stitches. These harked back to nineteenth century bags and fitted in with the whimsical novelty designs that were popular in the 1950s. Paris and Vienna were key centres of production for the finer examples of such bags. Inferior versions were produced until the 1970s, and tend to be machine made and lined in lesser quality fabric.

Rigid, lady-like handbags made from leather or faux leather were used by women of all ages in the 1950s. Mappin and Webb, for example, produced classic British-made bags in supple leather and lizard skin. These were often paired with elegant suits and co-ordinated hats and gloves. This trend continued right up until the 1980s, albeit for an older and more reserved generation (think Margaret Thatcher). The crème de la crème of daytime handbags, similar in style,

was the Hermés Kelly bag. This was known until 1955 as the Hermés, but was re-named the Kelly in homage to Grace Kelly's marriage to Prince Rainier of Monaco.

The 1960s saw the reign of the shiny plastic handbag – plastic was fantastic! This could mean a vinyl bag imitating patent leather or a malleable bag that was more obviously plastic.

Conversely, in the late 60s and early 70s, there was a return to more natural fabrics for bags. The homemade aesthetic was big again, with crochet, beaded and macramé bags seeing a huge resurgence. Carpet bags, which borrowed from Edwardian styles, became hugely popular and came in Mary Poppins-esque proportions.

Evening bags in the 1970s returned to a glitzy deco-inspired aesthetic. This meant 20s-style pouch bags, expanding bags (originally a Victorian creation), and glittering statement clutches inspired by the 1974 release of the film *The Great Gatsby*, demonstrating how popular culture so often influences fashion.

The 1980s was the decade of the designer bag, whether it was Chanel, Louis Vuitton, Moschino or Gucci – the bigger the logo the better!

Opposite: A selection of skin bags demonstrating the overlap in styles from the 1930s to the 70s Examples include springbok, crocodile, snake and alligator.

QUICK ERA GUIDE

20s – Miniature and hand-held, or fabric with ornate carved handles

30s – Sleek structured skins with interesting clasps

40s – Sturdy, sensible and long lasting – also baskets

50s – Novelty box bags and lady-like rigid handbags

60s – Plastic fantastic

70s – Oversized carpet bags and craft influences. Small and sparkling for night

80s – Elaborate designer or cheap and 'matchy matchy'

This page: Simone holds a highly collectible 1940s telephone cord bag. Stacked up her wrist are a selection of Bakelite and Fakelite bangles.

cactus flowers

glitterbugs

BRAND SPOTLIGHT

ENID COLLINS

Enid Collins bags and their many copies are amongst the most recognisable bags of the mid twentieth century. There were two types of bags primarily made by this company: a hard wooden box bag and a linen bucket-type bag. Both types are instantly identifiable by their ornate decorations, executed with paint, sequins and rhinestones. Their motifs often reference nature.

But why do you see so many copies of Collins' famous bags? From the late 1960s onwards the firm produced 'Sophistikits' that enabled customers to produce their own Enid Collins-look rhinestone-covered bags. In good condition these are equally sought-after.

There are a number of different types of Enid Collins bags. Those marked "E.C." were produced when Collins was still running the company. Those produced after Enid sold the company in 1970, have the horse logo, and are marked "Collins", but not "Enid".

Opposite: These two Enid Collins handbags demonstrate both a design by Collins herself, bottom, and a licenced design, top.

Right: Enid Collins linen shopping tote, with colourful flowers and strap handles.

'*A beautiful bag is like a beautiful sculpture — you have to admire it.*'

Emma Longstaff, handbag collector

WHITING AND DAVIS

Whiting and Davis began their company in 1876, producing metal-mesh bags modelled on nineteenth century reticules. These bags that had once been very expensive, and handmade in gold or silver, became eminently more affordable once machine processes came in in 1912. It is important to note that Whiting and Davis are still producing their bags today, this means you can still pick up decent vintage-looking bags from them, but watch out if you think you are buying an older example, it might not be as old as you think.

HERMÉS' BIRKIN BAG

Legend goes that actress/singer Jane Birkin and Jean-Louis Dumas (Hermés' CEO) were on the same flight in 1984 when Birkin happened to accidentally empty the contents of her bag onto the floor. This resulted in a discussion: Birkin wanted the perfect weekend bag and, in great detail, described exactly what it should look like and what it should include. And thus the iconic Birkin was born.

Above: Hermés magazine advert from 2012.

Opposite: Two 1950s American metal-weave handbags, both with Lucite lids and handles.

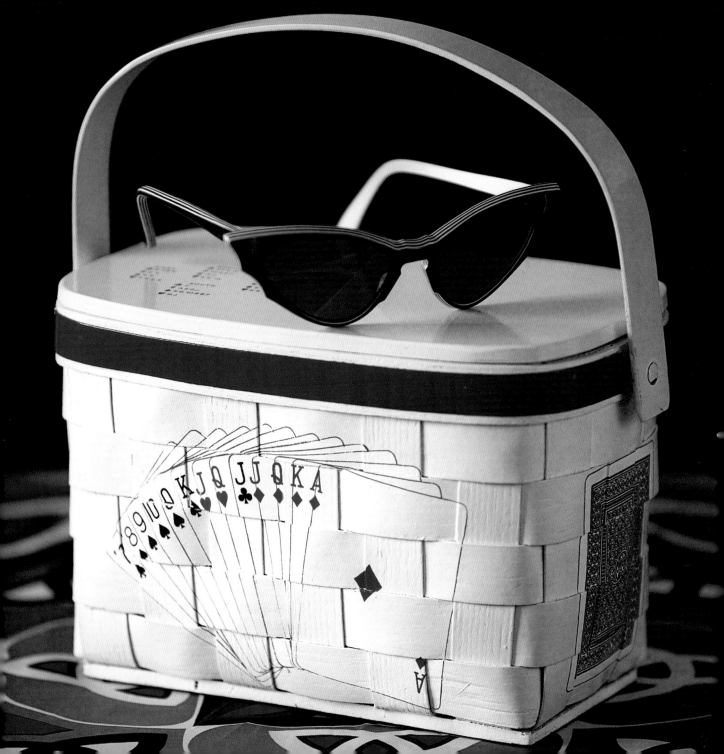

Designers to look out for

- Koret
- Gaitan
- Jane Shilton
- Enid Collins
- Waldy bag
- Corde
- Mappin and Webb
- Llewyln
- Dorset Rex
- Whiting and Davis
- Wilardy
- Launer (Queen Elizabeth's favourite bags!)
- Caro-Nan
- Glomesh

Opposite: Many of the best 1950s novelty bags come from America. This example, printed with playing cards and lined in quilted cotton, is by Caro-Nan.

Right: Magazine clutch. 1970s. Modern versions of these can be picked up, printed with recent magazine covers.

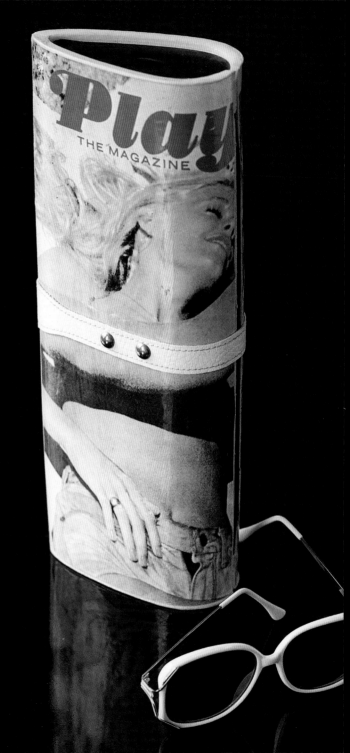

Eyewear

*'To me, eyewear goes way beyond being a prescription.
It's like makeup. It's the most incredible accessory.
The shape of a frame or the colour of lenses can
change your whole appearance.'*

Vera Wang

Throughout the twentieth century it was noticeable that a change in decade brought about a change in eyewear design. This was most apparent with sunglasses. Initially a purely practical item, their importance as a fashion accessory soon overtook their pragmatic beginnings.

In our opinion, creative eyewear design pretty much halted in the 1990s. In keeping with the unisex fads of the decade a deluge of rather ubiquitous sporty styles became fashionable (Oakley, anyone?). The early noughties' bought with it a smattering of bling, which was then followed by ten years of aping the entire back catalogue of the last eighty years. Every style, at some point, has made a return to the spotlight, often following the trends in era-inspired clothing. Major brands cottoned on and re-issued their archive designs, allowing wearers to ensure that their modern copies conformed to current eye safety regulations.

Types and Styles of Eyewear

- Sunglasses
- Eyeglasses
- Lorgnette
- Monocle
- Pince-nez
- Winged
- Aviator
- Bug Eye
- Cat Eye
- Wraparound
- Oversized
- Round
- Rectangular

HISTORY

The development of sunglasses from functional item into the status symbol that they are today is an extremely interesting one. Fundamental to their proliferation was the discovery of the harmful effects of ultra-violet rays from the sun on our eyes. This was found to particularly affect those working in the military, direct sunlight or heavy industry during the latter part of the nineteenth century.

Early twentieth-century interest in elite leisure activities, specifically concentrated around motoring and aviation, created a new high-end market for protective sungoggles. Subsequently, as sunglasses found more leisure-based uses, such as for outdoor sports, the designs moved away from the unattractive, yet practical, goggle, towards a more attractive spectacle-like design, utilised by the European and American glitterati while on holiday in the European Riviera. Images of the rich and famous wearing these glasses filtered down through the fashion and style magazines such as *Vogue* and *Harper's Bazaar*, bolstering consumer demand.

Despite this, it was not until 1929, in Atlantic City, that Sam Foster (later of Foster Grant Sunglasses) saw a market for cheaply produced sunglasses to cater for the newly emerging consumer market. Utilising the manufacturing techniques for, by then out-dated, celluloid hair combs, he produced cheap plastic frames to encase tinted glass lenses. Almost overnight, these became hugely popular. Film stars of the day were photographed wearing them and demand grew for more innovative shapes, styles and colours.

Left: These hand-held folding glasses are *lorgnettes*. The name derives from the French *lorgner* 'to take a side-long look at'. This pair were made in the 1950s and are encrusted with rhinestones.

Opposite: A pair of rare 1930s round sunglasses, made in England, with their original glass lenses. Note the irridescent tint to the glass.

TOP TIP
Look out for rare
sets of plastic 'cat's
eye' sunglasses with
interchangeable
detachable frames.

Right: Sharon wears a pair of
1950s cat's eye sunglasses with
marcasite trim to the edges
of the frames.

Opposite: These 1950s cat's
eye sunglasses are one of the
most elaborate pairs we have
seen and are French-made.

EXPERT: KATHERINE HIGGINS, BBC TV VINTAGE EXPERT, BROADCASTER AND AUTHOR

Memories of childhood... we all have them and mine revolve around sunglasses. Practically from birth I identified my mother not by her clothes but by her sunglasses. As I grew, so did those sunglasses, moving from the lightweight metal Polaroids of the 1960s to the flamboyant giant butterfly frames of the 1970s (her beloved Correna Photomatics), which matched their slogan, "so original, so futuristic, in fact, so beautiful".

Spotting authentic vintage is all about handling. Mineral lenses (ie: glass), predominately used from the 1930s into the 1960s, have a noticeably heavier feel than today's plastic lenses. There is also something reassuringly solid about pre- and post-war frames. Look closely at the hinges; they shouldn't be lightweight, flimsy or gleaming. Early on, plastic was die-cut (rather than injection-moulded) and finished to perfection, which your fingertips will learn to identify. Examine the sides, bridge and lenses, as they may carry some sort of maker's details.

www.katherinehiggins.co.uk

Frames for reading glasses followed suit in the 1950s. Up to this point, spectacles and reading glasses were mainly encased in sensible wire frames. Now you could buy jazzy plastic frames, not unlike those available for sunglasses – even metal-rimmed glasses became more ornate and were often carved and inlaid with rhinestones. For those with less flamboyant tastes, a simple heavy rim in a classic design contributed just as much to the iconic looks of the era.

Whilst the 1950s was the decade of the frame, in the 60s the lens had equal footing. Sunglasses grew in size and lenses were made with a variety of colours and effects. The humble reading glass didn't quite go so far.

Opposite: A trio of English-made mid-century plastic sunnies. The top two pairs are both unbranded deadstock. The bottom pair are 'Cool-Ray' by Polaroid.

Next page: These 1960s orange sunglasses are the epitomy of pyschedelic style.

By the 1970s both sunglasses and reading glasses had reached their largest - they covered half the face, and whilst this generated a number of iconic sunglass designs that are still very popular today, this design didn't quite take off with reading glasses. It was during this decade that Australia introduced the world's first national standards for sunglasses to ensure a uniform level of safety. However, brands such as Persol and Polaroid had been consistently producing highly protective lenses since their inception, in 1917 and 1937 respectively.

QUICK ERA GUIDE

20s–40s — Predominantly rounded. Some use of plastics for frames. Lenses often made of glass

50s — Cat's eye or winged

60s — Bug-eye or rectangular

70s — Oversized. Sunglasses sometimes rimless

80s — Softened exaggerated cat's eye. The dominance of Ray-Bans and their imitations

BRAND SPOTLIGHT

RAY-BAN

The 1980s was the decade of Ray-Ban sunglasses. Ray-Ban (to banish rays) were first produced by Bausch and Lomb in 1937. Their sunglasses had been particularly popular in the 1950s and 1960s, but this petered out somewhat in the 1970s. The turnaround came in 1982 when Ray-Ban signed a $50,000-a-year deal with Unique Product Placement to put their sunglasses in television shows and films. Ray-Ban sunglasses appeared in over 60 films per year between 1982 and 1987. The 1980 film *The Blues Brothers* is often credited with returning the Ray-Ban Wayfarer to popularity (first created in 1952) but this didn't translate into consumer sales until 1983.

TOP TIP

The market is currently flooded with fake Ray-Bans. The real deal has 'BL' (pre 1998) or 'RB' (post 1998) etched – not painted – onto either one or both lenses.

Brands to look out for

- Ray-Ban
  (Bausch and Lomb)
- Oliver Goldsmith
- Polaroid
- Persol
- Linda Farrow
- Correna Photomatix
- Foster Grant
- Cutler and Gross
- Metzler
- Michele Lamy

Opposite: 1980s tortoiseshell Ray-Ban 'Caballeros' and a pair of modern Ray-Ban 'Wayfarers'.

CLAIRE GOLDSMITH, FOR OLIVER GOLDSMITH

Founded in 1926 and a family-run business for over 80 years, Oliver Goldsmith has become a primary source for contemporary sunglasses. OG revolutionised the eyewear industry not only by creating frames that protected your eyes, but also by making eyewear a fashion statement. Dress designers, royalty and celebrities, such as Audrey Hepburn and Michael Caine, approached the brand to make eyewear for them and history was made. Today, the company is run by Claire Goldsmith (Oliver's great-granddaughter) and is still synonymous with stars and style. Beautiful handmade replicas of the original designs are available to buy, from 'The Manhattan' (*Breakfast at Tiffany's*) to Peter Seller's favourite, 'The Vice Consul', there is a style for everyone.

Claire says:

1. Research your brands – price is not a reflection of quality. Look to independent companies, not just for the frames, but also for optician services. The quality of frame and level of service you will receive will definitely be worth it.

2. The best way to clean your glasses is to use lukewarm water and some washing up liquid. Give them a wash, rinse, and polish with a clean soft cloth – done!

3. My grandfather used to say 'I don't believe in theories about a certain style suiting a certain shape of face. Life is too short to worry about such things. If you find a shape you like, have it!'

4. Always ask your optician to fit your frames for you – your frames shouldn't slip down your nose or fall off. A well-adjusted frame will make all the difference. Remember to do this a few times a year, keep them clean and in a good box, and your frames should last you a lifetime.

Opposite: Chunky Oliver Goldmith frames from the 60s.

Left: Goldsmith's iconic 'Manhatten' frames, as worn by Audrey Hepburn in *Breakfast at Tiffany's*.

Scarves

'A casual thing a scarf, but what a blessing, it can be when one knows where and how to wear it.'

Dorothy Stote, *The Bride's Book*, 1938

Scarves have never really gone out of fashion. What has evolved is the way we wear them. Today one might tie a scarf to a handbag to brighten up an outfit or even, if a scarf is particularly large, fashion it into a top. A single scarf can be the most versatile vintage fashion accessory you can buy. Quality can be instantly ascertained by touch, which makes for easy rummaging. Vintage scarves are still easy to find, though price and value vary greatly. A choice piece can be worn, framed or simply enjoyed as part of a collection.

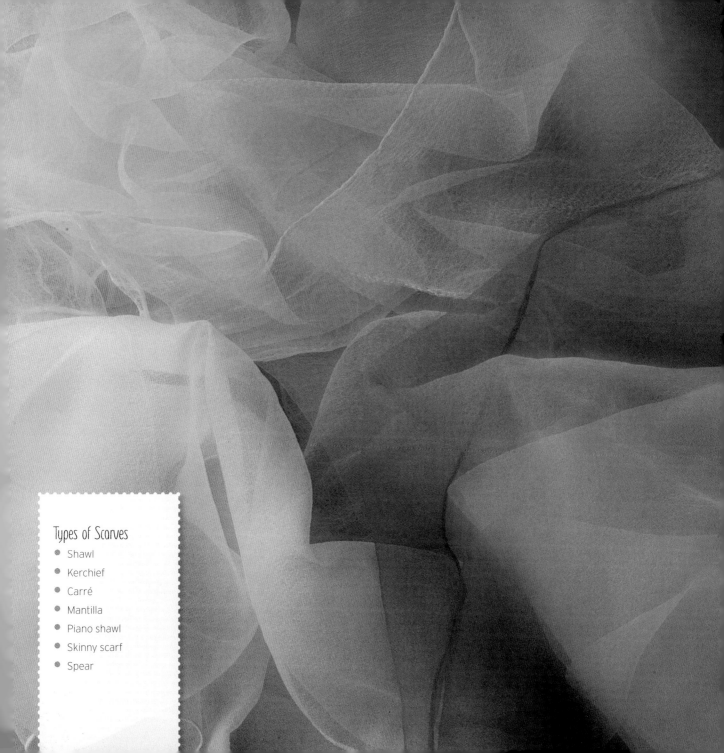

Types of Scarves
- Shawl
- Kerchief
- Carré
- Mantilla
- Piano shawl
- Skinny scarf
- Spear

HISTORY

As a fashion accessory the scarf is a twentieth-century phenomenon, coming into its own in the 1920s. Scarves, as we know them today, were buoyed in popularity by the rise of commercial silkscreen printing, which led to smaller square scarves and long, thin scarves being produced in abundance. The dancer Isadora Duncan was known for her flowing scarves that fitted with the slim tubular lines of dresses in the 20s (although she tragically died after such a scarf became entangled around the wheel and axle of her open top car, breaking her neck). Throughout the 20s and 30s, scarves were often printed with geometric art deco motifs in bold, contrasting colours. Scarves were not only manufactured in silks, but also in rayon a popular synthetic alternative also known as 'art silk'. In contrast to these delicate scarves, large enswathing piano shawls made from fine-fringed silk and mantillas (a type of Spanish lace shawl) were popular for both day and evening.

Patriotism was the order of the day in the 1940s and many scarves featured propaganda heavy designs making them an important part of the war effort – it was an easy way to show your support. These were produced in America by Echo (one of the first American manufacturers to print its brand name on scarves), and in Britain by Jacqmar. Such scarves today are highly collectible, and often feature the flags of the allied nations.

Page 123: A selection of sheer featherweight chiffon scarves, popular in the 1950s for tying over hair rollers.

Right: A smart navy 1960s bag accessorised with a Richard Allan geometric silk scarf (of the same era) and finished with a 1980s pearl and glass statement earring in place of a brooch. Naomi purchased all three items from a carboot/ yard sale for just £3. Combined in this way they make a more expensive looking item.

Opposite: Hand-painted scarf of buttery gold silk with black fringing, purchased in Greece in the 1950s. The bottom image shows the fine detail of the painting.

Left: A selection of bows fashioned from (l to r) a silk 1930s spear scarf, a 70s harlequin pattern spear scarf and the cheeky inclusion of a 70s cravat. Spear scarves were hugely popular in the 30s and again in the 70s as part of the Deco revival.

Opposite: A scarf from the 1937 Paris Exposition Internationale, dedicated to art and technology in modern life. The flags represent the nations that took part. (N.B: From 1935-45 the German national flag featured the Nazi emblem; the swastika.)

Delicate wisps of sheer mono-coloured chiffon or nylon, tied kerchief-style at the neck were fashionable in the 1950s. Scarves of this decade are typified by fun, exuberant novelty designs in cheerful bright colours. Grace Kelly became an icon of scarf wearing in the 50s, looking effortlessly chic in scarves worn tied around the neck or head. In 1956 when Kelly broke her arm she even used a Hermés scarf as a sling.

Bold psychedelic motifs printed on square and triangular scarves were the height of fashion in the 1960s, taking design inspiration from Op Art. Emilio Pucci scarves from this period are particularly sought-after. Pucci began producing scarves in 1949 and was often inspired by his underwater photography. He considered his scarf designs equally as important as those of his clothes.

Shawls were a central part of the hippy look of the late 1960s and 70s. Huge fringed or crochet shawls were often worn and could be draped over the shoulders or worn sarong-style, tied at the waist. For those after a more glam look, metallic lame scarves were tied in big bows to complement equally glitzy outfits. This same style was worn on the head (again in a bow) in the 1980s.

In the 80s, designer scarves, with highly visible company logos, were the height of fashion. This trend has continued to date as many designers realised the commercial value and ease that comes with creating logo and brand-based scarves.

DATING TIP

Whilst scarf shapes and sizes are not necessarily tied into era, the material tends to be. Earlier scarves were more commonly made of natural materials.

BRAND SPOTLIGHT

LIBERTY

British-brand Liberty scarves are very collectable. They were particularly popular throughout the 1950s, with Robert Stewart, one of the leading lights of textile design, designing for them. They have also produced some enormously useful video tutorials on scarf tying, see www.liberty.co.uk/fcp/content/liberty-tv/newsarchive

Below: A late 1930s Liberty print design on 'golden bird' silk.

JACQMAR

Jacqmar scarves feature some of the most distinctive prints one can find on a square of silk. Founded in 1932 by Joseph 'Jack' Lyons and his wife Mary, Jacqmar began as a prestigious fashion house and only started producing their iconic scarves in the late 1930s to use up off-cuts of silk used for garments. The most collectible scarves tend to be those designed by Arnold Lever, particularly the patriotic scarves he designed for the company during World War II, first produced in 1941.

Opposite: A variety of silk scarves with floral designs by famed textile firm, Jacqmar, 1955.

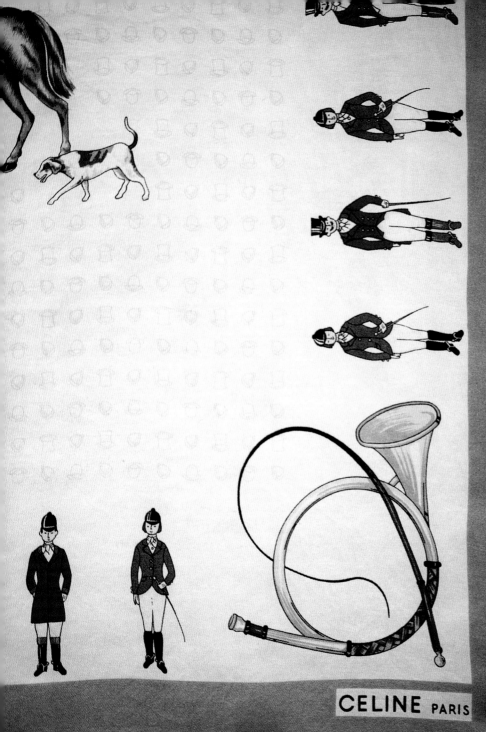

CELINE PARIS

'My mother always said to me "keep your style simple and accessorise well." Nothing is better than a scarf to achieve this.'

Sharon Selzer

Left: Equestrian-themed scarves have been produced throughout the 20th century, and are sturdily collectable. This is a 1980s Celine version.

Opposite: A novelty promenanding print scarf, typical of cheery 1950s scarf design.

Labels to look out for

- Etro
- Liberty
- Jacqmar
- Hermés
- Vera
- Ascher
- Echo
- Moschino
- Richard Allan
- Pucci
- Kreier
- Monique Martin

Left: A complete 1970s Mappin and Webb trio, consisting of a long silk scarf, handbag and purse in a matching geometric print.

Opposite:
Top left: A 1950s daschund printed scarf, originally owned by Liz's Great Grandma.

Top right: A modern Laura Ashley scarf, based on their original 'Pelham' scarf, designed in 1954.
The design is named after the company's first store on Pelham Street, London.

Below right: A scarf commemorating the Queen's coronation in 1953.

Below left: A 1980s Las Vegas hotels souvenir scarf.

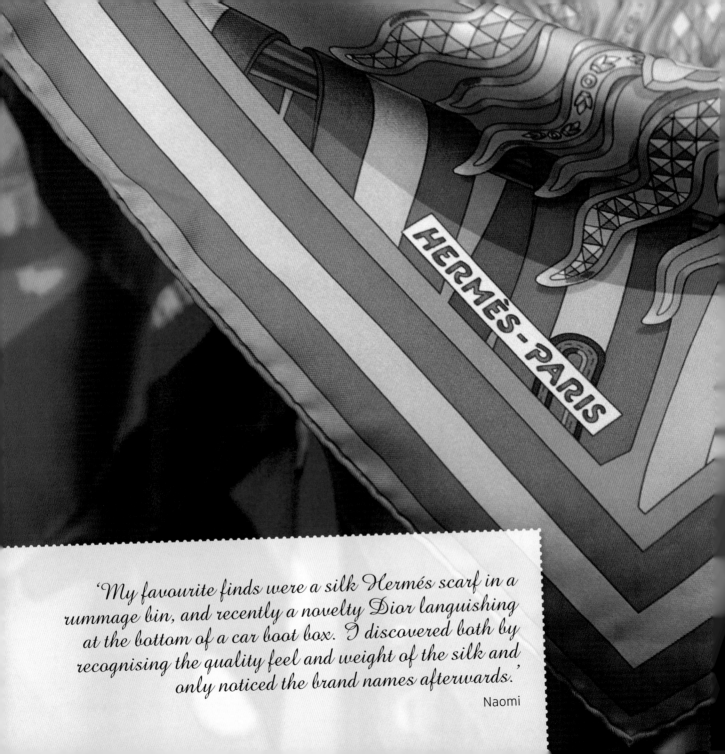

'My favourite finds were a silk Hermés scarf in a rummage bin, and recently a novelty Dior languishing at the bottom of a car boot box. I discovered both by recognising the quality feel and weight of the silk and only noticed the brand names afterwards.'

Naomi

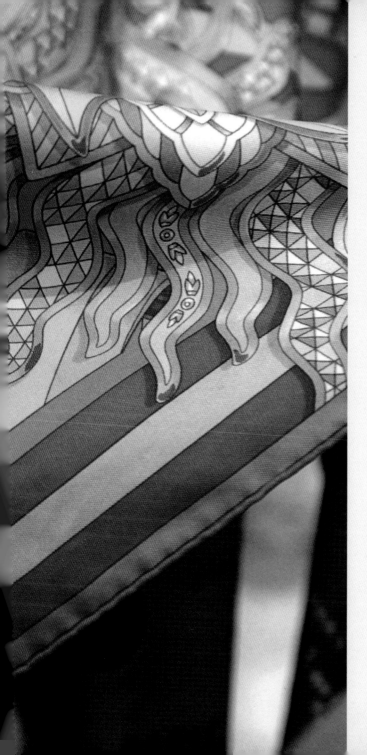

BRAND SPOTLIGHT

HERMÉS

The Hermés company, first established in 1837, didn't start producing their famous scarves until the 1930s. Many of these are now considered design classics and, as such, retain their value well. Hermés started off as a leather goods and saddle maker (hence the equestrian theme to many Hermés scarves). Their first scarf, produced in 1937, was called 'Jeu des Omnibus et Dames Blanches', or white ladies surrounded by horse-drawn buses. A classic Hermés scarf is a square measuring 90 x 90cm, and weighs approximately 63g. Anything different is an indicator of a lesser forgery.

Left: Close up, it is possible to appreciate the quality of craftsmanship that goes into producing a Hermés scarf. The craftsmen print each of the colours making up the design in turn (frame-by-frame) according to a very precise sequence. Notable artists who produced designs for Hermés include Jean-Louis Clerc and Xavier de Poret.

Vintage Miscellany

This chapter is dedicated to some of the more obscure vintage paraphernalia that was once popular, but has now become lost in the annals of time.

What follows is by no means an exhaustive list and you may want to consider adding any number of finishing touches to your outfit, where desired. For instance add an interesting metal work or carved belt buckle to a plain fabric belt, carry a decorative paper, fabric or feather fan or even finish off a look with a cigarette holder or cheroot.

SOME OF OUR FAVOURITE EXTRAS

HOSIERY

The correct hosiery is essential if you are going for a period-accurate look. As a rule of thumb, seamed, or fully-fashioned stockings are for the 1930s, 40s and early 50s looks only. For an authentic look choose a nude coloured stocking with a tan seam. Though this is not a hard and fast rule. Most vintage girls would agree that What Katie Did (available globally) provide the broadest and most affordable range of reproduction stockings.

The 1920s and post-60s are a seam no-go. The exception to the rule, as ever, are the 80s when companies like Wolford brought back the seamed stocking. This was also the decade of the legging, sheer black 15 denier stockings and rather lacy patterned creations.

It's a misconception that coloured hosiery is a modern day invention. Coloured stockings were particularly in favour in the 1920s and 30s but have in fact been worn for centuries. White tights became fashionable in the 1960s whilst the 70s saw a colourful explosion in tights.

'My favourite modern styling tip is to match thick bright tights to a scarf or your hat, especially a turban.'

Naomi

138

Hosiery labels to look out for

- Bear Brand
- Pretty Polly
- Pamela Mann
- Wolford
- Dior

Page 137: Kigu hand-held ashtray and ladies' engraved cigarette holder from the early 60s.

Opposite: Red leather platform shoes from 1949. Also featured are the original (and quite racy for the time) stockings, with red clocks and seams that the original owner wore with them.

COMPACTS

Vintage compacts are highly collectable – generally, the more ornate, the higher the value. These tiny feats of engineering were often given as gifts and came in soft pouches to protect their decoration. Plainer examples are often initialled. Whipping out a vintage compact makes reapplying your lipstick so much more satisfying.

TOP TIP

Whilst the vintage make-up in a compact case may look appealing we would highly recommend *against* using it. Vintage cosmetics contained lots of nasty chemicals that we would not want to be putting on our faces today!

Compact labels to look out for

- Stratton
- Zell
- Kigu
- Gwenda
- Vogue Vanities
- Volupte

PARASOLS AND UMBRELLAS

A tightly rolled umbrella doubling as an ornate walking stick will lend an air of sophistication to any outfit, but works especially in harmony with a sharply tailored suit. Parasols have cropped up in the history of fashion more times than we can mention. In a twentieth century context, paper parasols were en vogue from the 1920s onwards (a trend pilfered from longstanding Asian cultures). This extended to fabric and lace in the 1950s when they were used to complete both Rockabilly and Tiki looks. Moribund by the 1960s, they last made a frothy reappearance during the Edwardian revival of the 1970s. Unfortunately, many early paper and silk versions have perished over the years. Though often the real beauty and craftsmanship lies in the handle: Glittering Lucite, animal heads carved into wood, ivory or early plastics and clean art deco shapes in Bakelite are not uncommon. An umbrella stand of attractive examples can make an elegant home display.

TOP TIP

Look out for Fox's Paragon umbrellas. These are considered the crème de la crème of British-made umbrellas and are still exported worldwide.

STOLES AND MUFFS

A stole was an essential accompaniment to an evening or cocktail gown until the 1960s. Superior versions will have hidden pockets, nestled inside or outside the stole. Apart from a place to rest your hands this also added weight, ensuring the stole hung as it should.

While we do not endorse the fur trade, it is an undeniable part of early vintage fashions. Many real fur stoles are still in circulation, though these can be in a wide variety of conditions. Faux fur has actually been around since the late 1920s, though it really came into its own in the 1950s. A good example is Astraka. A less controversial alternative to fur, real or otherwise, would be a velvet, silk or beaded net capelet.

The lesser-spotted muff is simply a hollow tube designed to keep ones hands warm. A muff therefore is a great alternative to winter gloves. Muffs come in a wide variety of fabrics, generally fur (astrakhan and ermine) although they can also be seen in velvet, embroidered silks and occasionally even feathers. Many muffs also double-up as handbags, containing a concealed pocket or an integrated purse at the back. They can be hung round the neck by a ribbon or cord, though this is not an essential.

If you do buy fur, make sure any product you purchase is CITES exempt. CITES is the Convention on International Trade in Endangered Species of Wild Fauna and Flora and governs what furs and skins can be legally traded, both new and old.

Above: Leopard cloche hat by Gardenia and Albert Hart ocelot muff, 1949.

Labels to look out for

- Astraka *'beauty without cruelty'* – a synthetic version of Astrakan or Persian lamb, a controversial (the best is said to be foetal fur) yet popular fur, recognisable by its tight dark curls.

CARDIGAN AND COLLAR CLIPS

Cardigan or 'sweater' clips are a nifty 50s invention for securing your knitwear neatly around your shoulders. They are formed by two clip fastenings, generally quite ornate, linked with a chain. The clips can be attached to the top corners or edges of a cardigan turning the garment into a 'cape', meaning the shoulders and back can be covered whilst arms are exposed. This look works particularly well with a pencil skirt and blouse and evokes the elegant style of the 1950s. It's also a good way to show off armfuls of bangles.

NAOMI'S TIP

Cardigan clips are my favourite forgotten accessory. They add a touch of unrivalled chic to an outfit and always attract compliments. Original ones are fairly rare these days, but like shoe clips, the lesser-spotted cardigan clip has seen a huge resurgence in popularity, especially amongst the craft crowd. Like shoe clips they can be fashioned using a pair of (strong) clip-on earrings: simply attach a chain between the two and clip on. Other alternatives include using pins, or attaching clips to buttons or bows. For heavier garments, two secure brooches work best. Smaller versions can also be attached to collars to be worn instead of a necklace. This last look can also be achieved by stitching buttons to your collar, as demonstrated in the picture here, or by attaching metal collar tips.

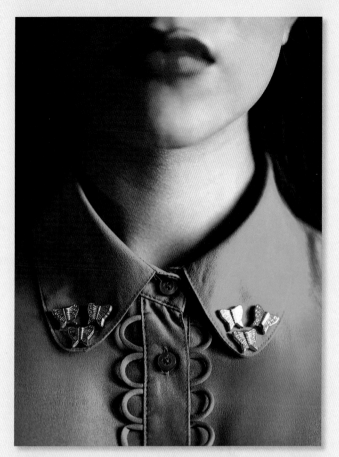

Liz and Naomi's Buying Guide

They say knowledge is everything, but there is no substitute for experience. Whether you are building a serious collection or just buying for fun, the pitfalls can be the same. This guide, based entirely on our own experiences as long-term vintage addicts, will help you maximise and hone your purchasing powers.

SHOES

✳ **It is notoriously difficult to judge the fit of vintage shoes.** They often come in a range of strange sizes like 55 or 60 and fittings such as AAA to A, B or C. It is almost impossible to chart these sizes and fittings into a homogenised modern day equivalent. Thankfully, most vendors now list shoes in terms of inches and centimetres, some will try and allocate a modern size to their shoes: if in doubt just ask for the measurements. As well as measuring your own feet take note of the dimensions of your most comfortable shoes (i.e. measure the inside).

✳ **Online shoe buying is high-risk.** It is impossible to judge if the shank has been damaged. If it has, it will make the shoe 'bend' under the weight of the wearer in a way that makes it nigh on impossible to walk. The shank runs between the heel and the outersole and sits under the arch of the foot. The only way to minimise this risk is to shop with reputable sellers who have a returns policy.

✳ **In older shoes always check** the buckles, fastenings and straps, as these are the first parts to perish.

LIZ'S COLLECTORS' TIP

If shoes are being sent in their original box, request that the seller does not sellotape the box. I've had a number of disappointing occasions where I had to damage an original shoe box to get a pair of shoes out.

JEWELLERY

✳ **Be aware** that some online sellers use the same vintage boxes as props for all their stock images. This can make a piece appear to be older and of greater collectability. It can also, falsely, insinuate a particular brand or value. Scroll through an entire set of listings if you suspect this is the case and it will soon become apparent. These types of sales normally state 'box not included'.

✳ **Ensure the clips of vintage earrings** are still strong enough to stay on your ears; this is not an easy fault to fix. On this note, pierced ears for women were the norm from the late 60s onwards and not before.

✳ **It is easy to get carried away** upon discovering an interesting novelty piece, so examine it carefully for tarnished surfaces, scratches or missing stones. Check all hinges, fastenings and links for weak spots. Good quality items often feature a security chain.

✳ **Ask before trying any items of jewellery on.** We've known dealers get rather antsy about trying on even clip earrings. Jewellery may look indestructible but can often be more fragile than it appears.

BAGS

✳ **Always check the fastenings of a vintage bag.** Sometimes it is worth putting a few of your own items inside it to check that the clasp will remain fastened with the added weight. Clasps on vintage bags are often difficult to repair so this is particularly important if you require the bag for general use.

✳ **Always ask if you can see the inside of handbags.** Check for deteriorating linings and damaged hinges.

✳ **Always remember:** older, carved plastic frames have a tendency to snap.

GLASSES

✳ **If you do decide to go full vintage**, try to buy deadstock items (unworn since the day they were made) to ensure that there is minimal damage to the lenses.

✳ **It is also possible now to have lenses replaced**, tested and adjusted in both vintage eyeglasses and sunglasses. A number of specialist companies have sprung up to cater for this demand.

✳ **With plastic box bags avoid anything** with crazing, fogging or a vinegary smell.

✳ **The 20s/30s-style revival of the 1970's** resurrected a number of popular bag designs of the Deco era (think reticules, chain mail and other small pouches), often with the addition of a long shoulder strap versus a small chain link one. Long straps were not a common bag feature pre-1970 so this will help date a bag.

✳ **Carved frames**, mainly fashioned out of bone or plastic, can add huge value to an early beaded or cloth bag, depending on how intricate the detailing is. The most collectable we have come across is the painted Pierrot motif. Many collectors will buy these frames regardless of the state or existence of the bag.

NAOMI'S BUYING TIP

Always try on sunglasses before buying, to make sure the frames haven't warped. Importantly this also allows you to check for prescription lenses which could damage your sight. If you are unsure whether your sunnies conform to modern safety regulations due to age or scratching only wear them for cosmetic purposes - it's not worth the risk!

GLOVES

HOW TO SIZE VINTAGE GLOVES

✳ **Buying the right size vintage gloves like shoes can be a tricky process,** but these simple steps should make it easier to judge your glove size. Locate the widest part on your palm and run the tape measure all the way around that part of your hand. This measurement, when taken in inches, should roughly correspond to your glove size. For example, hand measurement = seven inches = glove size seven.

If you have particularly long/short fingers, it is always worth also measuring from the tip of your middle finger to your wrist - normally the two measurements are roughly the same. It is important to use the hand you write with for this measurement, as this hand is likely to be bigger. This tip is a much better way of judging glove size than by simply using your shoe size, as suggested by some sources. Until the 1970s there was a rough correlation between US shoe size and glove size (glove sizing is the same internationally), meaning you could guess your glove size according to shoe size although today this is no longer a hard and fast rule, as it seems glove sizes have also become susceptible to vanity sizing.

HATS

✳ **Hats from the 1960s tend to come up small.** This can be attributed to the focus on younger fashions.

✳ **Felt hats are prone to moths** - at the first signs of eggs or larvae, remove the offending critters, and freeze the hat (ideally in a plastic bag) to destroy any remaining eggs.

✳ **Check that the inner headband is not too mucky.**

SCARVES

✳ **Sadly, scarves are often relegated to the rummage bin;** so let your hands lead your eyes, the weight and grain are both indicators of a superior find. Handle a few different scarves and you will soon get to know the difference.

✳ **Our absolute top tip is to look out for hand-rolled and stitched edges.** This is a sure fire sign of quality.

UMBRELLAS & PARASOLS

✳ **It is not unreasonable to ask to see a fully opened specimen.** Always ask the vendor or dealer to do this for you, as damage can often occur upon opening. Check in a strong light for signs of thinning, moth or splits in the fabric. Another common issue is fading. Long furled examples will have bleached on the outside whilst retaining their original hue or pattern inside.

FUR & SKIN

✳ **Supple is the key word when it comes to buying leather goods.** Cracked and dried leather is best avoided – it makes for rigid, inflexible and painful shoes, or broken straps and handles in bags. Skin purses past their best will flake a snowstorm of scales. Good skin accessories should have retained a glossy sheen.

✳ **Should you choose to go down the real fur route** avoid anything that emits a strong odour or is visibly malting. A musty smell is particularly challenging to remove.

✳ **A well-preserved fur of superior quality will have just as much attention paid to the lining.** Think thick satin often embroidered with a lady's initials. The fur should have retained its shine and should be free from bald patches or matting.

Shopping for Vintage

Ah. We love to shop. Though we both have quite different styles. And the way we shop has changed in the last few years. Building a relationship with a small number of niche shops can often result in a call out of the blue to say a special something has been arrived, and they are holding it for you. An example of fantastic customer service. However, too many shops these days have very defined ideas of price and style. This is exactly what an over saturated market requires and provides simplicity for consumers who don't necessarily know what they want. For the rest of us though it has somewhat taken away the thrill of the hunt. To remedy this, we have both returned to basics.

NAOMI'S TIPS

I've gone back to the car boots and second hand sales I loved in my youth. Living on the south coast in a historic naval town, I still have ample opportunity to attend house clearances, jumble sales and the odd auction (the traditionally aged populations of seaside towns means these are frequent). In the summer months, the town is swamped with fêtes, country fairs and traditional English summer events. Even our local allotments host a summer gathering complete with cream teas and bric-a-brac stalls.

I still love a charity shop but I find most of them are now so overpriced when it comes to clothing (remember not *everything* old is vintage). This book partly came about through my new love of buying accessories. They seem to have missed the price hike. This year alone I have found three Bakelite bangles in second hand shops. No washing or moths to contend with either!

LIZ'S TIPS

When hunting for vintage accessories I always head straight for antiques centres. I spent my late teens and twenties dividing my time between London, Yorkshire and Hampshire and have hunted out great antiques centres in all three areas. My top three for UK readers: Kingston Antiques Centre (Surrey), Salisbury Antiques Centre (Wiltshire) and Montpellier Mews Antiques Market (Harrogate). I find that antiques centres offer more vintage oddities and are generally fairer priced than vintage stores. This is particularly true if you are hunting for early twentieth century pieces. The majority of pre-1940s bags in my collection have come from antiques centres.

OUR FAVOURITE SHOPS

ANYTHING GOES
97 Elm Grove, Southsea, Hampshire PO5 1LH
This south coast boutique also travels around the UK festival scene in a specially converted horsewagon. Natasha Gibson's 70s clothing is a favourite with Daisy Lowe and Florence Welch and she stocks modern Navajo jewellery.

CLOBBER, POKESDOWN, BOURNEMOUTH
www.vintageclobber.com
Head to Clobber for a fantastic selection of accessories; particularly shoes from the 20s-80s.

ELEGANT ERA, HARROGATE, NORTH YORKSHIRE
www.elegantera.com
Amazing pre-1950s accessories, including a huge array of very collectible compacts.

MELA MELA VINTAGE, TEDDINGTON, MIDDLESEX
www.melamela.co.uk
Mela Mela specialise in mid-twentieth century vintage. Their jewellery offerings are particularly superb.

SPACE
2 Rue De La Grand Armée 13001 Marseille,France
Hidden behind Marseille's Métro Réformes this small shop reveals itself to be a plastic deadstock mecca, from 20s celluloid hair combs and immaculate cat's eye sunglasses, to trays of never-worn bangles from 3 euros.

TANGO TEA
3 Albert Rd, Southsea, Hampshire, PO5 2SE, UK
Art Deco and accessory heaven. Suppliers of the lorgnettes on page 110.

THE LOOKING GLASS, BRIDGNORTH, SHROPSHIRE.
www.thelookingglass.co.uk
The Looking glass is best known for their incredible stock of 1950s dresses but they also sell an incredible selection of hats and modern Dent's evening gloves, perfect for adding that final touch to your outfit.

THE VINTAGE EMPORIUM, BRICK LANE, EAST LONDON
www.vintageemporiumcafe.com
Equally known for its numerous (and immaculate) 1920s dresses as it is for owner Oli's addiction to pre-1950's hats.

THE SHOP/SELZER, CHESHIRE STREET, EAST LONDON.
www.theshopvintage.wordpress.com
The place to go for gloves, scarves, hats and costume jewellery from the second half of the twentieth century.

HUNKY DORY VINTAGE
226, Brick Lane, London E1 6SA
A mecca for good 60s/70s leather bags and original sunglasses.

OUR FAVOURITE ONLINE VINTAGE RETAILERS

1940S SWEETHEART
www.etsy.com/shop/1940sweetheart
For vintage shoes, many in larger sizes.

DEAD MEN'S SPEX
www.deadmensspex.com
Original vintage spectacles.

HAPPY FELLA
www.ebay.co.uk/usr/happy-fella
For the best in vintage pre-1950s handbags.

MADAM'S VINTAGE
www.madamsvintage.com
For vintage spectacles.

POPPYCOCK VINTAGE
www.etsy.com/shop/PoppycockVintage
Vintage hats galore.

STELLA ROSE VINTAGE
www.etsy.com/shop/stellarosevintage
Handpicked shoes from Melanie Nute.

VINTAGEHOARDS
www.etsy.com/shop/VintageHoards
Novelty print nut Rachel always has a fantastic selection of 1950s bags.

WILLIAM CASSIE
www.ebay.co.uk/sch/williamcassie/m.html
Incredible vintage hats by the likes of Jack McConnell.

PASSIONATE ABOUT VINTAGE
www.passionateaboutvintage.co.uk
Stocks a range of original vintage designer jewellery, from the 1920s-60s, by the likes of Trifari, Weiss and Hattie Carnegie.

LOVELY'S VINTAGE EMPORIUM
lovelys-vintage-emporium.myshopify.com
Clothes and accessories from international stylist and editor Lynette Peck. Great for 70s and 80s bling.

ALEXANDRA VINTAGE
www.alexandravintage.com
Alexandra Dewis has the dual talent of being just as good at picking accessories as she is at choosing frocks. Visit her studio in Reading or buy direct from her website.

MODERN REPRODUCTION AND FUTURE COLLECTABLES

The aim of this book is to provide information for both collectors and those interested in vintage style and, as such, good modern reproductions have earned their place in our tome. We are also fond of modern pieces by indie designers who have put their own creative touch to an old design. These are the collectables of the future.

ABBIE WALSH
www.abbiewalsh.com
Abbie Walsh creates exquisite one-off accessories from vintage fabrics and embellishments

AGNES AND NORMAN
www.agnesandnorman.co.uk
Handcrafted shoes

ALICE EDGELEY
www.edgeley.com.au
Bespoke millinery (see turban on p.23)

AMANDA FATHERAZI
www.amandafatherazi.com
From boudoir dolls to collaborations with Charlotte Olympia, Amanda's creations lie somewhere between art and fashion.

AMERICAN DUCHESS
www.american-duchess.com
Historical repro footwear and purveyors of shoe clip hardware

BETSY HATTER
www.betsyhatter.co.uk
Bespoke vintage-inspired and costume hats

B MILLINERY
www.bmillinery.com
Millinery taking inspiration from fashions of the 1920s to 1960s with an exciting modern twist

JEEPERS PEEPERS
www.jeeperspeepersretro.co.uk
Vintage-inspired glasses and sunglasses

KARINA'S BAGS
www.karinasbags.co.uk
Handmade leather handbags

LULU GUINNESS
www.luluguinness.com
Quirky handbags which have become instant collectables

LUXULITE
www.etsy.com/shop/Luxulite
Sparkling modern Lucite jewellery

MISS L FIRE
www.misslfire.com
Vintage inspired shoes and handbags with a touch of quirkiness

NAN'S KNITWEAR
www.facebook.com/nansknitwear
Handknitted turbans

NAOMI TATE
www.naomitate.com
Naomi Tate sources treasures from the past to create heirlooms for the future

NOW VOYAGER
www.now-voyager.co.uk
Handmade vintage-inspired hair accessories

PIP JOLLEY
www.pipjolley.com
A luxury jewellery brand inspired by and infatuated with the last 60 years of style, art and culture

REMIX
www.remixvintageshoes.com
Faithful reproductions of shoes from the 1920s to 50s

ROCKET ORIGINALS
www.rocketoriginals.co.uk
1940s and 50s inspired shoes made mostly from vintage patterns

SWEDISH HASBEENS
www.swedishhasbeens.com
Based on 1970s clogs, Swedish Hasbeens have become hugely popular with vintage-loving ladies

TATTY DEVINE
www.tattydevine.com
Tatty Devine are best known for their Perspex jewellery, but also produce incredible sunglasses

THE VANITY CASE
www.etsy.com/uk/shop/TheVanityCase
Hand painted personalised fans by Sadie Doherty

WHAT KATIE DID
www.whatkatiedid.com
For the best repro stockings

YOU FLAMING BRUTE
www.etsy.com/shop/youflamingbrute
Hand carved Perspex and moulded resin from South coast designer Julia de Klerk

Opposite: These pieces come from Pip Jolley's Rollerette collection, inspired by the glamour of the 1950s and the ritual of setting your hair every night.

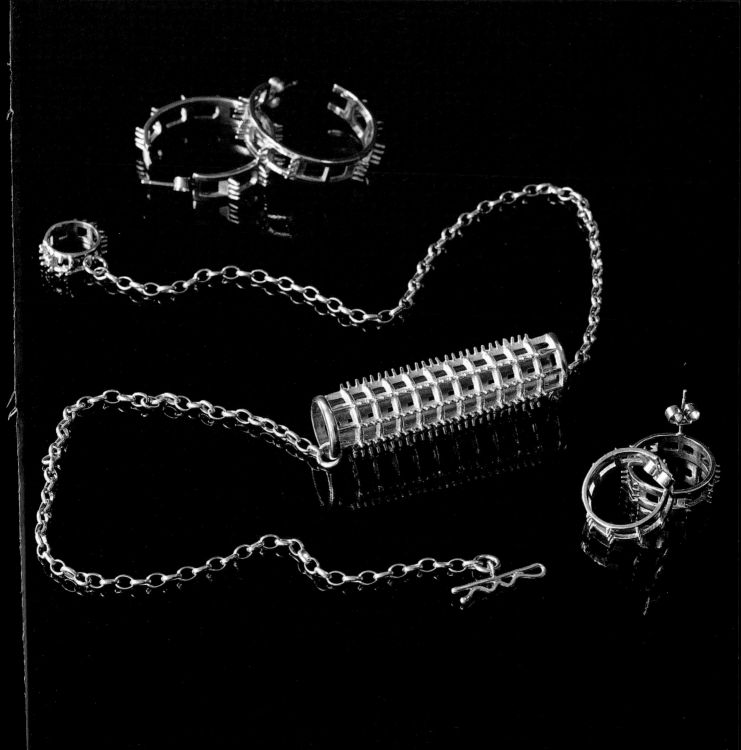

Opposite: A pair of couture cuffs by Naomi Tate, made with authentic 19th century velvet and cut steel decorations, backed on silk.

Left: Tatty Devine put a completely new spin on traditional cat's eye sunglasses with these incredible eyelash examples.

FURTHER READING AND RESEARCH

BLOGS WE LIKE

www.advancedstyle.blogspot.co.uk
Seriously chic mature ladies.

www.sheepandchick.blogspot.co.uk
Jealousy-inducing shoes are the mainstay of
Tracy Dolphin's amazing vintage collection.

www.emmapeelpants.wordpress.com
1960s and 70s expert Liz Eggleston regularly
posts marvelous magazine editorials featuring
vintage accessories.

www.thevintagevanitycase.blogspot.co.uk
Sadie is the lady behind our fabulous Style Me
Vintage fan, and writes a fabulous blog too.

www.miamai.co.uk
The home of Portsmouth-based artist, illustrator
and designer Ami Lowman, who also created our
cameo illustration on p.82.

www.missturnstiles.co.uk
Vintage hyper-glamour, served up by our model
Simone Hadfield.

PLACES TO VISIT IN THE REAL WORLD

HAT WORKS MUSEUM, STOCKPORT
www.stockport.gov.uk/hatworks
The UK's only museum dedicated to the hatting
industry, hats and headwear.

MUSEO SALVATORE FERRAGAMO, FLORENCE
www.museoferragamo.it
A museum focusing on the production of Italian
footwear designer Salvatore Ferragamo.

NORTHAMPTON MUSEUM, NORTHAMPTON
www.northampton.gov.uk/museumcollections
For the largest collection of shoe heritage in
the world.

SIMONE HANDBAG MUSEUM, SEOUL, SOUTH KOREA
www.simonehandbagmuseum.co.kr
A Korean museum that, rather fabulously, is
housed in a building shaped like a handbag.

THE BATA SHOE MUSEUM TORONTO, ONTARIO
www.batashoemuseum.ca
Showcasing 4,500 years of shoe history.

THE FAN MUSEUM, GREENWICH, LONDON
www.thefanmuseum.org.uk
The Fan Museum is the UK's only museum devoted
entirely to every aspect of fans and fan making.

**THE MUSEUM OF BAGS AND PURSES,
AMSTERDAM, THE NETHERLANDS**
www.museumofbagsandpurses.com
For a wide variety of handbags from around
the world.

THE SHOE MUSEUM, STREET, SOMERSET
**www.somersetroutes.co.uk/site/the-shoe-
museum**
Showcasing the history of British brand Clarks.

ACKNOWLEDGEMENTS AND THANKS

Naomi:

I would like to thank Jessica and Julia from the Southsea Santander bank branch, who probably provided me more moral support and actual help than most. I also owe huge thanks to Howard Thompson (official SMVA chauffeur), Frances Thompson (for the loans and inspiration), Margaret Chester, Jean Thompson, Jill Firman (my aunt and quite the 70s fashionista, for the use of her hatboxes), Akeela Bhattay, Hanson Leatherby, Zoe Crosby at Oliver Goldsmith, Miriam McDonald, Emma Hollands and Sally Tonkin at Laura Ashley Southsea for their invaluable support and input in wallpaper related styling, Kate Allchin, Emma Oakley and Sarah Sandiford at Laura Ashley Coms, and of course my Al and my Lydia for whom I did this book. I also thought a lot about Dave when making this. Thank you for the laughs and taking the mick out of my book ideas. I miss you.

Liz:

I would like to thank my Mum, Elaine Tregenza for starting my whole obsession with collecting vintage in charity shops all those years ago. Turns out all that top tat wasn't such tat after all.

We would both like to thank the following people:

Rebecca Winfield, our marvellous agent (www.davidluxtonassociates.co.uk). Emily Preece-Morrison at Pavilion, for sharing our editorial vision and making this book happen. Brent Darby for taking exactly the images we had in our heads and Kristy Noble for being an all-round stellar assistant. We loved working with you two #ATeam. Katherine Higgins for being utterly fabulous as always and a huge inspiration. Liz and Terry De Havilland for the insight and encouragement. Amber Butchart (www.theatreoffashion.co.uk) for your excellent selection of turbans and for your support and generosity. Andrew, Freddie and Genevieve at Cornelia James for being such amazing sports. Georgina Abbott at Atelier Millinery for her fine interview. Claire Goldsmith for her insight and fine tips. Natasha Gibson for letting us pilfer her shop. Sadie Doherty for making us the Style Me Vintage Fan – so amazing! Natalie Leon for her expert words, amazing loans and shoot styling skills. Sharon Trickett for being a gorgeous model and nail artiste extraordinaire. Simone Hadfield and Susannah Mollah (plucked off the street by Liz!) for being stunning models, and Gemma Court for making them (and us!) look stunning. Sharon and Michael Selzer for solid advice and scarf insight, plus Laura and Chloe at The Shop. Ami Lowman for the stunning hand-drawn frames used in our cameo montage - you are one talented lady. Abbie Walsh for her 40s floral headband and general loveliness.

PICTURE CREDITS

All special photography by Brent Darby except those credited below.

©: p.1: Mary Evans/Peter & Dawn Cope Collection; pp.2, 3: Hanson Leatherby; p.10: Illustrated London News Ltd/Mary Evans; p.14 Hulton Archive/Getty Images; p.18: Image Courtesy of The Advertising Archives; p.19t: Time & Life Pictures/Getty Images; p.19b: Bettman/Corbis; p.22: Illustrated London News Ltd/Mary Evans; p.26: Mary Evans/Everett Collection; p.28: courtesy of Atelier Millinery; p.32: Mary Evans/National Magazine Company; p.36: Mary Evans/National Magazine Company; pp.40-41: courtesy of Cornelia James; p.42: Condé Nast Archive/Corbis; p.43: Condé Nast Archive/Corbis; p.49: Image Courtesy of The Advertising Archives; p.64: V&A Images/Alamy; p.65 courtesy of Terry de Havilland; p.68t: Everett Collection Historical/Alamy; p.71b: Mary Evans/Peter & Dawn Cope Collection; p.80: Image Courtesy of The Advertising Archives; p.88 Hulton Archive/Getty Images; p.103: Mirco De Cet/Alamy; p.104: Image Courtesy of The Advertising Archives; p.120: Photos 12/Alamy; p.121: courtesy of Oliver Goldsmith; p.128: Mary Evans/Peter & Dawn Cope Collection; p.129: Illustrated London News Ltd/Mary Evans; p.134 AFP/Getty Images; p.142: Mary Evans/National Magazine Company; p.143b: courtesy of Lauren Southam; p.144: Mary Evans/Peter & Dawn Cope Collection; p.150: Mary Evans/Peter & Dawn Cope Collection.

Loans

Elena Medin and Roberta Fedora for the divine Enid Collins Cactus bag.

Miss L Fire (www.misslfire.co.uk) for the Cinderella shoes.

Rachel Wilkie (www.etsy.com/shop/vintagehoards) for the huge box of shoes, bags and hats and also her unfailing support along the way.

Tatty Devine (www.tattydevine.com) for the wonderful sunglasses.

Gemma Fairlie at Majorie May Vintage (www.majoriemayvintage.com) for her grandmother's cocktail ring.

Research

Elizabeth Coulson (elizabeth.coulson@network.rca.ac.uk)

Make-up

Gemma Court (gemmacourt.carbonmade.com)

Nails

Sharon @ Minnie Moons (www.minniemoons.com)

Models

Susannah Mollah (susannahsayssew.blogspot.co.uk)

Simone Hadfield (miss-turnstiles.blogspot.com)

First published in the United Kingdom in 2014 by
Pavilion Books Company Ltd
1 Gower Street, London WC1E 6HD

"Style Me Vintage" is a registered trademark of Pavilion Books

Text © Naomi Thompson and Liz Tregenza, 2014
Design and layout © Pavilion Books, 2014
Photography © Pavilion Books, except those listed in Picture Credits

Commissioning editor: Emily Preece-Morrison
Designer: Sophie Yamamoto
Photographer: Brent Darby

ISBN: 978-1-90981-500-1

A CIP catalogue record for this book is available from the British Library.

Colour reproduction by Rival Colour Ltd., UK
Printed and bound by Toppan Leefung Printing Ltd., China

This book can be ordered direct from the publisher at
www.pavilionbooks.com

10 9 8 7 6 5 4 3 2 1

ALSO AVAILABLE FROM PAVILION BOOKS:

Style Me Vintage: Hair by Belinda Hay, ISBN 978-1-86205-902-3
Style Me Vintage: Make-up by Katie Reynolds, ISBN 978-1-86205-918-4
Style Me Vintage: Clothes by Naomi Thompson, ISBN 978-1-86205-936-8
Style Me Vintage: Tea Parties by Betty Blythe, ISBN 978-1-86205-973-3
Style Me Vintage: Lookbook, ISBN 978-1-86205-976-4

Naomi Thompson is the author of *Style Me Vintage: Clothes*.
She is a stylist, vintage addict and professional treasure
hunter. She has featured on BBC 4 *Woman's Hour* and in
pretty much every glossy in the UK, regularly contributes to
Homes and Antiques magazine and has a legion of online
fans that follow her second hand adventures.
@imoantweets

Liz Tregenza is a vintage fashion specialist and historian,
and recently graduated with a Masters in Design History from
the RCA. Liz has worked for a number of museums including
Hampshire museums service and the V&A. She co-curated
her first museum show at the age of 20 and has since
contributed to numerous books and research papers. Liz is
an avid collector of all things novelty.